THE CARER'S COMPANION

A WINSLOW GUIDE TO CARING AT HOME

THE CARER'S COMPANION

RICHARD CORNEY

WINSLOW

First published in 1994 by
Winslow Press Ltd, Telford Road, Bicester, Oxon OX6 0TS, UK
Reprinted 1995

Copyright © Richard Corney, 1994

All rights reserved. No part of this publication may be reproduced, stored in a retrieval system, or transmitted in any form or by any means, electronic, mechanical, photocopying, recording, or otherwise, without prior permission in writing from the copyright owner.

02–1722/Printed in the United Kingdom

British Library Cataloguing in Publication Data
Corney, Richard
    Carer's Companion: Winslow Guide to
    Caring at Home
    I. Title
    362.14

ISBN 0-86388-131-9

Contents

Acknowledgements • viii

Introduction • ix

(1) Hearing the Diagnosis • 1

(2) Disabilities Explained • 4

Dementia • 4
Early Signs • 6
Alzheimer's Disease • 8
Multi-Infarct or Arteriosclerotic Dementia • 10
Parkinson's Disease • 11
Huntington's Chorea • 13
Dementia: an Overview • 14

Stroke • 16
Immediate Effects • 16
Following Stroke • 18

Depression • 20

3 A Difficult Journey • 24

Dementia • 25
Stroke • 31
Depression • 35
Common Threads • 39

4 Coping Practically • 41

Helpful Personnel • 42
Your Health • 48
Breaks and Respite Care • 50
Minimizing Risk in the Home • 53
Financial Help • 53
Financial Provision for the Future • 56
Legal Arrangements • 56

5 Coping Emotionally • 59

Having Sufficient Practical Support • 59
Having Sufficient Emotional Support • 60
Setting Realistic Standards for Caring • 63
How Realistic is it Emotionally for
   You to be Caring for this Person? • 66
Recognizing that Feelings are Getting
   out of Control • 68
Coping: a Summary of Principles • 69

6 Practical Problems • 70

First Principles • 70
Dignity • 72
Avoiding Confrontation • 73
Encouraging Independence • 74
Minimizing Stress • 75

Adapting • 76

Typical Problems • 76
Forgetfulness • 78
Difficulty in Performing Simple Daily Activities • 86
Clinging, Following and Wandering • 87
Insomnia • 89
Hearing Hurtful Things and Facing Aggression • 92
Incontinence and Toileting Difficulties • 96
Sexual Problems • 102
Depression • 120
Stroke • 126

⑦ The Carer's Journey • 134
In the Beginning • 134
The Carer's Grief • 135
When the Caring Ends • 142

⑧ Letting Go • 144

Appendix I *Useful Organizations* • 150

Appendix II *Helpful Books* • 154

Index • 156

Acknowledgements

The author expresses his thanks to his colleagues Karen Mason, Deidre Lund and Linda Jones for their encouragement and help with this book. Dr Graham Stokes, consulting editor for Winslow Press, made numerous helpful suggestions in respect of the text. The author is also very grateful for the skilled and patient help of Sian Jones with typing the manuscript. Finally, a special thank you to the copy-editor, Tony Waterman.

Permission from David Higham Associates, London, to quote the Dylan Thomas poem, *Do Not Go Gentle Into That Good Night*, and from Oxford University Press to quote the Gerard Manley Hopkins untitled poem is also acknowledged.

Richard Corney has been working as a clinical psychologist for 15 years. He presently heads the psychology services for rehabilitation and the elderly for Clwydian Community Care Trust. The problems experienced by those caring for someone with a severe disability are an area of particular interest to Richard and he is actively involved both in research into the stress such carers face and in running carer support groups. He is married, has four children and lives in North Wales.

Introduction

THERE ARE at least six million carers in the United Kingdom, which translates to approximately 14 out of every 100 adults who are looking after someone who is mentally or physically disabled at home. About a quarter of these have been doing so for more than 10 years. Generally these carers are an unseen, silent and largely unappreciated group. Many are themselves elderly and not in the best of health. Government policy over recent years, echoing that of health service personnel, has favoured the provision of community-based services and the closure of long-stay hospitals. There are in fact excellent therapeutic reasons for this trend, which in its essentials is therefore to be encouraged. One possible effect of this policy, however, is to increase the burden of care that falls to family members, particularly if inadequate locally based respite facilities are available. When the bulk of care falls to the family, there can be clear benefits to the quality of life of the person being cared for: intimacy, the familiarity of home and loved ones, greater privacy and so on. The reality is that these advantages are often achieved at considerable cost to the carer, who may 'pay' in terms of both their physical and their emotional well-being.

A person disabled by a stroke or an illness such as Alzheimer's Disease or depression can present with problems that stretch even professional ingenuity and resources, and it is a tribute to carers that people typically show less disability when cared for at home than they do when cared for in hospital or a residential facility. This fact should not blind anyone to the cost that may be involved. This cost is complex, varying from simple financial considerations (one carer put this at £42,000 over five years) to ill-health, back problems, social isolation and psychological stress (research regularly demonstrates high levels of depression in carers). Taking the situation of an elderly person with dementia, a carer may be faced with constantly disturbed nights, outbursts of temper, incontinence, massive amounts of laundry, needing to help with the simplest of daily living activities such as washing, dressing and undressing, and severe restrictions in the ease with which they can get out and about. Sounds familiar? Yes, all parents of small children face these challenges. But, and here is the rub, the child does not weigh ten stone or more and usually returns your affection.

Caring for someone with serious disabilities can make it very difficult to get out and about, both socially and for everyday shopping needs. This can lead to acute feelings of isolation. Caring for a frail person is effectively a full-time job in itself, and many carers have to give up paid employment to do it. They can feel trapped at home in an unending grind of domestic chores and looking after an unresponsive and ungrateful person; no wonder that some research suggests that about a half of all carers feel that they are at breaking point. The wonder is that so many carry on as well as they do for so long. Recognition has been scant, not helped by the low 'glamour status' of the illnesses experienced by many of the people cared for. More recognition is beginning to come, fortunately, with increasing publicity about the difficulties that carers face. Increasing publicity or not, a large number of carers feel desperately alone with their problems.

This book is written to offer some support to those who are caring for someone suffering from a marked degree of mental disability. This would include people incapacitated by Alzheimer's Disease, other forms of dementia or a stroke, as well as serious psychological problems such as severe depression. The emphasis of this book, therefore, is toward carers who are looking after someone who is highly dependent on them through reason of their severe disability. This book aims to provide suggestions in a variety of areas, including the practical difficulties carers may face in their day-to-day living with the person they care for and, importantly, the feelings that may from time to time overwhelm anyone in this position.

This is not a book that needs to be read from cover to cover. As it attempts to meet the needs of people caring for individuals with a variety of disabilities, some sections will be redundant to a particular carer.

1

Hearing the Diagnosis

YOU MAY recently have heard that the person you are caring for or may have to care for has senile dementia or Alzheimer's Disease, or has had a serious stroke. These can be frightening terms: many people worry about 'going senile' more than they worry about death itself, and as for an illness with a name like Alzheimer's — well! The doctor who told you this may have looked rather serious, and talked apologetically of there being no cure. It is true that there is no cure for these conditions, but despite this a great deal can be done to reduce the difficulties experienced by those who have these conditions and, as important, to ease the difficulties facing those who have to care for the people who have them. This book is written to discuss the kind of help that is possible.

While the early part of this book is very much for those who have only recently been given a diagnosis (or indeed, those who have arrived at it themselves), it is not without relevance for those who have had a diagnosis and been caring for the affected person for years. This is because acceptance of or coming to terms with a condition like Alzheimer's Disease or senile dementia in someone you love is not an absolute 'either/or, you have or you haven't' business. Acceptance is a process that evolves over years, and involves many feelings of loss that we will talk about in some detail later. People can talk a little glibly about acceptance: "Of course, Mary has never accepted Joe's illness." Often it is not at all clear what is meant by this. Just what is Mary being asked to accept? Needless to say, she wants him well and not ill, and feels, to put it mildly, angry that he is not. This is wonderfully expressed by Dylan Thomas, writing about his ageing father's illness and failing eyesight:

Do Not Go Gentle into That Good Night

Do not go gentle into that good night,
Old age should burn and rave at close of day;
Rage, rage against the dying of the light.

Though wise men at their end know dark is right,
Because their words had forked no lightning they
Do not go gentle into that good night.

Good men, the last wave by, crying how bright
Their frail deeds might have danced in a green bay
Rage, rage against the dying of the light.

Wild men who caught and sang the sun in flight
And learn, too late, they grieved it on its way,
Do not go gentle into that good night.

Grave men, near death, who see with blinding sight
Blind eyes could blaze like meteors and be gay,
Rage, rage against the dying of the light.

And you, my father, there on the sad height,
Curse, bless, me now with your fierce tears, I pray.
Do not go gentle into that good night.
Rage, rage against the dying of the light.

A particular difficulty that Mary may have in accepting what is happening to Joe when he suffers from an illness like dementia is that there are such wide-ranging effects on his physical and mental wellbeing that these can at times seem to change him out of all recognition. What makes this viciously worse is a feeling of helplessness, a sense of being completely powerless to do anything about the illness and its consequences. This is a potent recipe for depression. It is hardly surprising that in this situation carers often embark on frantic searches for magic cures, potions and remedies; anything to feel less helpless, less at the mercy of the illness.

An important, practical way of feeling less helpless is to find out as much as you can about the illness or problem in the person you care for. It is equally important to learn about all the many things that can still be achieved in a rehabilitative sense, illness or not.

2
Disabilities Explained

Dementia

THE VERY word 'dementia', with its connotations of 'going senile', is powerfully negative. Some advocates of euthanasia advance this condition as a justification for their cause; pleading that even death is preferable. Early thinkers urged active measures to forestall the looming terror with which advancing age seemed inevitably associated. Born 106 years before the birth of Christ, Cicero wrote:

> It is our duty to resist old age; to compensate for its defects by a watchful care; to fight against it as we would fight against disease.... Much greater care is due to the mind and soul; for they, too, like lamps, grow dim with time, unless we keep them supplied with oil.... Intellectual activity gives buoyancy to the mind.... Old men retain their mental faculties provided their interest and application continue.

Most people would applaud the sentiments behind this; it is good to keep ourselves active both physically and mentally. One analytical psychologist, Carl Jung, saw the secret of old age as being to live as if you were immortal; thus if you are bored you had better do something about it! But Cicero, wise man though he was, lacked an important piece of information. In those days few people lived to be what would now be considered elderly. As recently as 1700 the average life expectancy for a man in England was 35 years, and even by 1840 this had only risen to 40-43 years. It has only been in this century that, if we discount the effect of wars, people may reasonably expect to end their days after the Biblical three score years and ten. And with these large numbers of elderly people came an important discovery: dementia was a condition affecting a minority, not all or even most of them.

So what exactly is dementia? Usage of the term has in fact changed since early days, and there are important types of dementia which differ from one another. These will be considered separately below. In general, however, dementia is:

1 An unhealthy condition of the brain (as distinct from a normally aged brain), which is acquired (that is, distinct from conditions present at birth, such as mental handicap). Some reasons for the condition are known, but in certain forms of dementia these reasons are as yet poorly understood.
2 A condition causing impairment of intellectual abilities, memory and the personality.

Dementia is *not* caused by old age; most elderly people do not become confused or 'senile', although statistically most people who suffer from dementia are elderly. It has been customary to talk of a condition of dementia affecting the under-65-year-old as 'presenile dementia', 65 years being a somewhat arbitrary cut-off point chosen because of pensionable age.

Early signs

The first, early signs of dementia can in fact develop a long time before any formal diagnosis of the condition is made. In part this is because the very early symptoms may be so subtle as to be hardly conspicuous, and anyway can simply be attributed to the normal process of ageing ("None of us are as young as we were") or seen kindly as a little developing eccentricity; in part, later on, it may result from the family's reluctance to accept that something *is* wrong and acknowledge this (to themselves as much as to the sufferer) by a visit to the doctor. In fact even family doctors can themselves contribute to this by a reluctance to involve specialist services, sometimes adopting a cautious 'wait and see' approach (and, in fairness to them, if they sent every possible sufferer from early dementia to these specialist services immediately, such services would be overwhelmed).

In the very early stages, carers see the person they care for as being 'different' in ways difficult to pinpoint. Families may comment that Mary is 'not the woman she used to be', and when pressed will talk about a loss of spontaneity — that she seems somehow less involved with life, less adaptable and capable. She seems less able to concentrate as she once did, and is beginning to lose interest in previously enjoyed activities. She has become very hesitant about making any kind of decision, preferring to leave all choices to others, and in fact often needs advice about trivia. Although this is difficult for them to put into words, they feel that Mary shows less emotion: previously a sensitive person who demonstrated and enjoyed affection, who was easily moved to tears on learning of another's misfortune, now she seems more in a world of her own. It has also become difficult to have much in the way of any real conversation with her and, previously a lady who took a real pride in the way she looked, she has become content to put on the same old dress day after day.

Increasingly obvious failings in memory are a common early feature of dementia (but do not signal its inevitable development). At first these episodes of forgetfulness may be hotly denied; later, as a degree of insight develops into the fact that intellect is not as it was, the person may become skilled at concealing the problem by evading questions or bluffing. On other occasions, when a lapse cannot be denied there may be an outburst of frustrated anger.

Quite commonly, though, the early picture is that of a concerned family while the person being cared for seems indifferent. Doctors are well used to consultations with an anxious family who bring along a bland, somewhat bewildered relative confused about all the fuss. And this blandness or detachment is in fact quite an important clinical sign that there may well *be* a problem in this context; the patient who comes independently to the surgery, actively complaining in their own right about concentration and memory not being what they were, is more likely to be suffering from something else entirely, such as stress, depression and so on.

We now consider the main causes of dementia.

Alzheimer's Disease

For the public, this name has in many respects become synonymous with senile dementia. With contemporary clinical diagnostic practice, Alzheimer's Disease is the largest group of 'the dementias', accounting for rather more than half of all dementia cases. Current estimates suggest that over 500,000 people in the UK suffer from Alzheimer's Disease. It is more common in the very old, but even in the over-eighties four out of five do not develop it.

The cause of Alzheimer's Disease is unknown, and in its early stages it is difficult to diagnose with any degree of certainty. In fact it is only possible to diagnose this condition definitely by a post-mortem examination of the brain, when the characteristic features of the brain disease can be seen. It tends to have an insidious onset, and early signs may include the person simply becoming somewhat eccentric or cantankerous.

The early stages are characterized by apathy, reduced initiative and problems with remembering. It is rare at this stage for the person involved to worry about things and to go to the doctor; it is far more likely that a spouse or relative will notice the loss of usual spontaneity and increasing forgetfulness, and themselves seek advice.

The difficulty for both doctors and families is that the problems seen in the early stages of Alzheimer's Disease are also seen in other conditions, most notably depression. For this very good reason, care is taken to exclude other plausible conditions that might account for these symptoms.

In the second stage of the disease, more serious intellectual deterioration and personality change develop. The person with Alzheimer's becomes more confused, forgets faces, has difficulty doing things with their hands and may show problems with speaking and understanding speech. The development of 'psychotic' symptoms such as delusional ideas may take place: for example, the idea that someone is spying on them, or is trying to poison them.

The final stages produce more severe neurological problems; the sufferer may be doubly incontinent, have fits and difficulty in walking. The disease ends in death. It is difficult to give precise estimates as to duration; some authorities argue that there are different forms of Alzheimer's Disease. A general working estimate is 10 years.

A great deal of research has been devoted to trying to identify the cause or causes of Alzheimer's Disease. As yet there are only promising lines of enquiry, no definite causes having been identified. Early concern about aluminium in the diet seems unfounded. Exciting current research is examining biochemical aspects (for example, the role of a beta-amyloid precursor protein). However, as implied above, the more research that is carried out on this illness the more there is a suspicion that the label 'Alzheimer's Disease' in all probability encompasses two, if not more, disorders. We know that there seems to be a genetic vulnerability, but this is small enough to mean that, even if a person has a close relative with the disease, that person is still unlikely to develop it. Alzheimer's Disease is prevalent among women, but this may be because the disease is more common in the very old and more women than men live to be very old.

Multi-Infarct or Arteriosclerotic Dementia

This accounts for about one in five cases of dementia; in a further one in five the person has both Alzheimer's Disease and Multi-Infarct Dementia. Multi-Infarct Dementia is the result of damage to areas of the brain caused either by a small blood vessel in the brain bursting, or by a clot forming in a blood vessel. This impedes blood flow to an area of brain which then dies. These two events are also what happens in a 'stroke' and, essentially, Multi-Infarct Dementia is caused by a series of 'mini strokes' damaging different areas of the brain in turn.

With this form of dementia, the background contributory factors are somewhat clearer. Persistent high blood pressure can make someone vulnerable and, because of this, a healthy life style may help to protect against this condition. In contrast to Alzheimer's Disease, in which women sufferers predominate, Multi-Infarct Dementia is slightly more common amongst men, possibly because of men being more vulnerable to circulatory problems.

In contrast to Alzheimer's Disease, the onset of Multi-Infarct Dementia may be judged with more precision ("You started having problems after you had that funny turn on holiday"). The course of this form of dementia is a fluctuating one, and the sufferer may well stabilize and show no deterioration for a period (or even regain some lost ground), only to deteriorate further as another 'infarct' occurs. A phrase commonly used to describe this deterioration is 'step-wise', in contrast to the slow, consistent, downward path seen in Alzheimer's Disease. This means that intellectual deficits tend to be more 'patchy' in this form of dementia, and the personality often remains relatively well preserved. People who suffer from this form of dementia, in contrast to someone with Alzheimer's Disease, usually present, at least in the early stages, with good insight, and may themselves be complaining about problems they are having ("I can't do sums like I used to"). Difficulties with memory are often clearly evident early on in this form of dementia, particularly a difficulty in laying down new long-term memories.

Parkinson's Disease

This, with its characteristic tremor and stiffness, is caused by a loss of nerve cells and the neurotransmitter dopamine in the area of the brain that controls movement. True dementia (in the sense of global impairment of intellectual skills) is less common in Parkinson's Disease than had previously been assumed, and in fact when Parkinson gave the condition his name he argued that intellectual deterioration was not a feature of this illness. Unfortunately a proportion of people suffering from Parkinson's Disease who do show a general dementia does seem to exist; the exact proportion is difficult to establish in that different studies have yielded varying estimates, but around 10 per cent is a working figure. Some authorities believe that there may be two different forms of Parkinson's Disease, which would account for differences in the incidence of dementia reported in this condition. Rather more people with Parkinson's Disease seem to show specific intellectual losses, for example a difficulty in switching attention from one topic to another. Where there is clear evidence of dementia, technically this is referred to as a 'subcortical dementia', which has certain clinical characteristics:

1 Impairment of memory.
2 An appreciable slowing in 'mental agility', particularly the ability to make use of knowledge that is there.
3 Emotional and personality change, very typically including apathy; outbursts of anger are occasionally seen.

In contrast to other forms of dementia, with Parkinson's Disease vocabulary and language skills are usually comparatively well preserved. Depression is a common feature (more common than dementia). Parkinson's Disease is relatively uncommon, with an incidence of fewer than one in a thousand for the general population, although it does become more common amongst older people, with an incidence of one in a hundred in over-65-year-olds. Mistakes in diagnosis are not uncommon in the early stages of this illness, before unmistakable features of gait and expression appear. Early 'stiffness' might, for example, be put down simply to 'arthritis'. Similarly, the slight tremor of the hands and feeling of general fatigue seen in the early stages tend to be worsened by stress, and consequently may be attributed to anxiety. Difficulty in writing is often the first noticeable problem.

The condition is treated (not cured) by drugs to modify dopamine levels in the brain. This treatment improves physical status and for a time may lead to an improvement in intellectual skills, where these have deteriorated, although this latter effect is short-lived. There have been some exciting developments in Italy treating severe tremor involving minor surgery and electrical stimulation, but this is some way from being universally available.

Huntington's Chorea

This illness is known world-wide and has a long history. It is likely that some of the women who were persecuted as witches in times gone by had this affliction. It is an important class of pre-senile dementia, with a typical age of onset between 35 and 40 years, though it may appear when the person is much younger (even below 10 years) and 10 per cent of cases occur in people in their sixties. It is a progressive illness, eventually characterized by jerking and writhing movements which become physically incapacitating. There is a marked dementia and the illness leads to death. Survival time depends on the age of the person when the illness developed: for children life expectancy is short, about six or seven years; for middle-aged adults, life expectancy is around 15 years.

The disease is inherited, with a 50 per cent risk to offspring at birth (although this figure decreases as the offspring grow older). The early signs are disturbance in behaviour and mood, followed by the characteristic choreiform movements and then dementia (although occasionally one may see different patterns). The early signs are often confused with other conditions or symptoms, such as alcoholic intoxication or a drinking problem. Suicide is a real risk amongst sufferers. Treatment is directed towards the relief of symptoms, and the major tranquillizers can be successful in alleviating the choreiform movements.

This is a particularly vicious illness, and family members have the added distress of wondering if they too are at risk. They now also have the appalling dilemma of deciding whether or not to have a test, which with reasonable reliability will show if they will develop the disease themselves. (This is an issue for blood relatives, not a spouse; the illness is not infectious.) It is an illness where both victim and family and carers need a lot of support, and no-one should have the test referred to above without prior counselling. There is an extremely helpful organization, Huntington's Disease Association (see address in Appendix I) which is an essential point of contact for sufferers of Huntington's Chorea and their families.

Dementia: An Overview

The above list covers the main categories, but is not exhaustive. It makes gloomy reading, with most sections making explicit reference to problems and life expectancy. This should not obscure the fact that much can be done to alleviate symptoms and reduce distress. When any person develops difficulties that suggest a major problem, a process should start which includes the following stages.

1. Thorough assessment

The word 'diagnosis' is deliberately avoided because, in the real world, a diagnosis is often arrived at on the balance of probabilities and by excluding other conditions. But the process of assessment should be thorough. Many elderly people become confused or display psychological problems when they have treatable physical conditions, for example, an infection. So the family doctor's surgery is the first port of call, where obvious physical problems will be excluded. The family doctor may need to then refer on to more specialist services, for example a geriatrician or psychogeriatrician, or clinical psychologist. (Chapter 4 begins by listing and describing the various professions that carers may need or come into contact with.) Nobody should accept serious intellectual and psychological difficulties developing as 'inevitable' without this assessment; all the conditions described in this chapter are illnesses or signs of illness, and not an inevitable consequence of growing old. A variety of tests may be arranged by specialist services, including brain scan (CT) and looking at electrical activity in the brain (EEG). It must be remembered that, although such tests help to clarify the picture, they are not conclusive; there is no 'test for Alzheimer's'.

2. Advice about management

None of the conditions described above are curable, alas; that, we hope, is for the future. But a great deal can be done, nonetheless — hence this book, and the importance of professional advice to go with it. Symptoms can be eased, distress minimized and, importantly, some problems overcome or better handled, or even eradicated as soon as they appear with the right approach to management.

3. Support for carers

No-one should be caring for somebody suffering from serious dementia without emotional and practical support, whether from family or professional sources. These needs are addressed in Chapters 4 and 5.

Stroke

Immediate Effects

Stroke is an emotive, frightening event, which can kill suddenly or leave someone severely disabled. The effect of stroke is sudden (hence the name), being obvious in seconds, minutes or, at most, hours. The brain, which controls all our thinking, speech and movement, depends on a constant supply of blood. If this is interrupted, even for a short while (more than four minutes), brain tissue dies. This blood supply can be interrupted because of a clot forming in one of the arteries feeding the brain or because a blood vessel in the brain bursts. Depending on the area of brain affected, a degree of disability occurs because that area of brain no longer works. The brain is effectively in two halves, rather like a walnut. There are various reasons for this, but in general terms one half of the brain controls the opposite side of the body. Commonly, in a stroke, one side of the brain is affected and the result is an apparent weakness on the other side of the body. As an example of this, a burst artery in the right half of the brain (a common site) will lead to an inability to move the left leg and left arm properly. The person who has had the stroke will be convinced that the problem lies in the arm or leg, perhaps describing it as 'weak' or 'stiff' or, very commonly, 'heavy'. In fact the problem is elsewhere; it is in the brain, which no longer sends out the appropriate messages to work the arms and legs properly. It is akin to a driver and motor car: the car is perfectly serviceable and in good order, but does not proceed because the driver has been taken ill and can no longer press the accelerator pedal or operate the gears correctly.

Loss of movement in the arm and leg on one side of the body (the arm is usually more severely affected than the leg) is referred to as hemiplegia; a less severe weakness of one side is known as hemiparesis. A degree of paralysis may also affect the stroke victim's face, which can cause difficulties with chewing, swallowing and the articulation of speech. Lessened control over the mouth can cause saliva to collect and drool out at the corner. Other problems can follow from a stroke. The person affected may no longer be able to speak properly, or may be able to speak but not understand speech; or they may have badly affected eye-sight.

Stroke is a common condition, to the point that most people will know of someone who has had one. It is most common in the elderly. In the UK, approximately 110,000 people have a stroke every year. It is in fact one of the commonest causes of death, but should not be confused with a heart attack, which, as the name implies, involves the heart and not the brain. The condition is known to be linked to certain risk factors, such as hypertension (high blood pressure), diabetes and heart disease. It should be noted, however, that all of these are only factors which increase susceptibility, even if you have one of these you will most likely not have a stroke. As noted, stroke is more common in the elderly, and is in fact rare before the age of 50.

Because of the above risk factors, some of which are linked to diet and healthy living, it is vital that some one who has had a stroke eats sensibly, does not smoke, exercises and has their blood pressure checked regularly, as these measures will reduce the chance of further, possibly even more disabling, strokes. The doctor involved may well prescribe medication to control blood pressure and/or aspirin to thin the blood.

Following Stroke

Depending on the severity of the stroke, there may be a degree of recovery; sometimes indeed this can be surprisingly good. With severe stroke damage, however, there may be little or none (very severe strokes kill people at the outset).

Strokes usually do most of the damage within the first 24 hours (occasionally this damage goes on developing for up to a week). Many stroke victims actually show improvement within 24 hours, some indeed recovering completely (although technically in this case they will have experienced a 'transient ischaemic attack' rather than a full-blown stroke). When fatal, a stroke is most likely to kill on the first day, but the risk of death does continue for about three weeks.

In general terms, recovery is fastest early on — in the days and weeks immediately following the stroke — and much slower thereafter (say after one month). As a general rule of thumb, little further recovery takes place after six months (save in the sense of continued learning how to adapt to and manage disabilities). This general guide as to the pace of recovery seems to hold true whatever the nature of the disability caused by the stroke. Where there is weakness on one side of the body, the affected leg generally improves before the arm, and also recovers more completely. Indications of limited recovery are:

1 loss of consciousness at the time of stroke;
2 severe paralysis (being unable, for example, to move one arm at all);
3 urinary incontinence immediately following the stroke, which persists for more than a few days;
4 loss of ability to see half the visual space (hemianopia).

Obviously a stroke may exacerbate pre-existing physical limitations, such as arthritis or circulatory problems. Treatment following a stroke is essentially rehabilitation, including physiotherapy to help reduce development of limb stiffness (through inactivity), speech therapy to help with communication difficulties (if present) and occupational therapy to encourage adaptation to disability. Medication may be prescribed to control circulatory problems and help minimize the chance of a further stroke. People who have visual difficulties following a stroke should see an orthoptist, who would make a thorough assessment of the exact nature of these difficulties and would then be able to advise about coping strategies.

It is not uncommon for people to become very depressed following a stroke. This may in part be 'physical', in that the brain has experienced a kind of physical assault, and in part emotional, as someone grieves for those things they can no longer do. This depression can become severe and, if persisting beyond what one would expect, given the nature of the loss experienced, will need active treatment in its own right.

It is also quite common for people who have recently had a stroke to be very emotional and to cry very easily, even if previously they have tended to keep a rather tight rein on their feelings. This tends to follow strokes affecting the left side of the brain; in contrast, someone whose stroke affected the right side of their brain tend to be more apathetic or surprisingly indifferent to their difficulties.

Depression

This is a word that has passed into everyday language: "I feel depressed today." Doctors and psychologists tend to use the word more specifically, however, preferring to reserve its use for a disabling condition which is beyond an everyday sad feeling. Someone who is clinically depressed is at the mercy of that low feeling, beyond the reach of everyday comfort and may fail to care adequately for themselves. As with any other clinical condition, depression varies in severity. In its most severe form a sufferer may take to their bed, seemingly completely apathetic, may be suicidal or have delusional ideas.

This condition is included here for three reasons. First, depression as a condition in its own right may be disabling the person you live with, and if this goes on for many months or years it is a wearying burden for you as carer. Second, it is not uncommon for people who are suffering from the early stages of dementia or who have had a recent stroke to become depressed, and thus have this as an added complication. Finally, if completely overwhelmed by the burden of caring (especially if unsupported), you as carer may become depressed.

Elderly people are particularly vulnerable to depression, with about 16 people in 100 experiencing it at some stage after the age of 65. Of these, two or three will be very seriously depressed. It is a condition that must be taken seriously; suicide is a real risk. As a group, the present generation of older people are, if a generalization may be permitted, less used to talking about emotional problems with a professional, and may see physical health problems as being the only legitimate concern to take to a doctor. Accordingly the early stages of depression are often undetected. With regard to the cause of depression, this is one of those situations in which there are almost as many theories as there are people putting forward ideas about it. A large number of these argue for a physical cause, in the sense of brain chemistry; others stress a history of adverse life experiences and disappointment, perhaps extending back to childhood. People clearly become seriously 'down' following personal trauma, such as a bereavement or loss of function following a stroke; what is not immediately clear is why only some remain depressed and unable to 'pick themselves up and start all over again', as the song goes. It is known that personal experience of major loss and bereavement is a potent factor. Another known 'risk factor' is that of helplessness, or feeling one is powerless to effect change in a life that is difficult in some ways, and thus feeling trapped with no way out of these difficulties. There are probably times in the life of every carer when this thought is around. Lack of an intimate confidant(e) and emotional support is also a common feature.

From a pragmatic point of view, someone who is depressed loses all zest for, and even interest in life. Appetite is jaded, sleep usually disturbed, with difficulty getting off to sleep and early waking (although, paradoxically, some depressed people sleep excessively) and loss of normal interest in a sexual relationship or usual hobbies. The feeling may be present that it is simply not worth getting out of bed. As noted above, feeling trapped is common and being depressed has been likened to feeling imprisoned — by the depression. Depression feels like a millstone round the neck; would that the sufferer could be shot of it (telling someone who is depressed to 'snap out of it' is manifestly unfair). An overwhelming feeling of lethargy and listlessness is common. In part this may come about because depressed people tend to cripple themselves with an impossible workload of 'things to do', often to impossibly high standards into the bargain. As the completion of all this is clearly impossible, not uncommonly depressed people do not even start, so everyday chores build up and up, fuelling the process. Importantly some of the symptoms of depression — being unable to concentrate and memory failings — mimic those early signs which can indicate a process of dementia. The term 'pseudo-dementia' is sometimes used to describe this clinical picture, which clearly illustrates the importance of skilled assessment so as to be clear about what the true nature of the problem is.

There is no shortage of ideas about treatment for depression, which vary from electro-convulsive therapy (ECT), to a veritable catalogue of anti-depressant medication, to an equally comprehensive list of psychological 'talking therapies'. And now for some good news: unlike the other conditions considered so far, here we can begin to talk in terms of outright cure. Depression is often (but not always) cured, most usually by a combination of treatment methods, which will be looked at in more detail in the section dealing with depression in Chapter 6. It often takes some considerable time to get this 'cocktail' or balance of treatment modalities right. Depression which is new and an isolated episode, as opposed to a life-long predisposition, is usually treated particularly successfully.

3
A Difficult Journey

IN ALL walks of life we can care most effectively after making some effort of imagination to put ourselves in the shoes of the person facing a particular difficulty: for example, what it might be like not to remember what you were told five minutes ago, or to be unable to understand speech and, moreover, to know there was a time when you did. This is the essence of empathy; in fact the root of the word is the notion of 'suffering with'; of course you may already feel you do plenty of this, albeit in a different way!

An effort to imagine what it must be like to have suffered a stroke, and be, for example, no longer able to move your hand or leg, or to speak, or what it might be like to suffer from dementia and have major difficulties with memory, concentration and control of your emotions will go some way to enabling you to respond objectively on occasion. By this I have in mind seeing some problems as the result of an illness or disability and not, for example, as coming from lack of motivation, laziness or simple rudeness. It may also provide ideas about how to respond to some of the difficulties with the person you care for.

Dementia

Maureen (not her real name) is a 72-year-old lady living with her husband in the small semi-detached house where they have lived for almost 50 years. She used to work as a chemist and after retiring became a best-selling author. Today, although she can no longer write because of her memory problems, she still has an IQ of 130, which shows her to have been a lady of high intelligence. She first experienced memory problems almost four years ago, but this situation has deteriorated more recently and is accompanied by significant weight loss and poor diet and sleep pattern. Below we have her account of the difficulties that have developed for her.

"I feel afraid, perpetually afraid of something, but I don't know what; even if I don't feel I've done something wrong, it's in the back of my mind that I've forgotten to do something, so I'm just so afraid all the time.

"I wake in the morning and nothing is familiar to me, I have to sit on the side of the bed and keep saying to myself, 'I know where I am, but it all looks wrong'; then you get used to it looking wrong and think 'Well, that's all right, that must be the way it is.'

"You see, I hide things, I put them in what I think is going to be a safe place, where only I will know where they are, and then I forget; then I spend most of the night moving around, trying to locate things. Where was it? Where did I put it? I can't remember, and then I realize I can't even remember what it was I was looking for, or why I was looking for it, so I go around the house moving things around hoping that something will trigger my memory and I will remember what it was I was looking for, but it doesn't.

"You see, if I'm wearing a blue skirt, I know I need blue shoes, and I know I must have them somewhere. So I start looking, but I can't find them and then I will forget what I'm looking for . . . just thinking about that now has brought me out in a cold sweat. I spend my whole life checking what I've done, in case I've done something stupid or dangerous . . . I'm so afraid all the time.

"My husband wants to go on holiday, but I don't want to leave this house. I want to stay here; I know here, and yet . . . I came down the stairs this morning and couldn't remember where the bathroom was, so I went back upstairs to look for it . . . stupid . . . stupid. I looked in the shower room, and of course, that wasn't it, I felt so stupid, so I just thought, 'OK, to hell with it' and I went back downstairs again and just happened to turn left . . . and there it was, the bathroom; and yet I wasn't really surprised to see it there, I was shocked and upset because I knew it was there, I'd just forgotten where to look for it.

"I sometimes wish 'Oh God, I wish it would end here, just stop now' but it doesn't, it goes on . . . then, I think, 'Well, I haven't done anything terribly wrong . . . I haven't burnt the house down yet, just so long as things don't get any worse'. I pray fervently that things don't get worse . . . but I don't think anyone hears, or else they're not listening . . . I must have been very bad.

"After, when I'm going upstairs to get something, I

pray, 'Please God, let me find it', but halfway up I have to sit down on the stairs and try and recall what I'm going for, but it's all gone again.

"I still try and cook a little, but the oven is usually filled with burnt offerings. You see, I set the timer to go off when the food will be ready; the timer goes off, but I've forgotten why the timer is on, so I turn it off, and forget about the food in the oven.

"I think I must be driving my husband mad. I can't deal with ordinary household things anymore, like paying bills; my husband has to do all that now or they wouldn't get paid . . . or get paid twice. It's not so bad for me, but it must be hell for him, you see he has a memory like an elephant, never forgets anything. He's in hospital now, and I feel so guilty that the stress I put him under has put him there . . . I really worry about that, and what I could or should do, but what can I do? Nothing. I wish there was something.

"The other day my daughter telephoned from Berlin. She said 'Hello mum, this is . . .' I couldn't remember who she was, it was like a door had shut me off. I could recall the voice, it was familiar, but the name, I couldn't put the name to the voice. It's humiliating. I don't feel angry, just despairing.

"I used to be an author; romantic novels. But I don't think I could even sustain a theme above two chapters now; it would take so long reading and rereading over what I'd written, and even then I would lose the thread. It wouldn't make any sense.

"The stupid thing is that I can remember childhood things. I can remember my mother plainly, like yesterday, and the big hats she used to love to wear; but I can't remember where I put the packet of Bisto, or what my husband has just said he will have for dinner. He says it's because I don't listen, but I do.

"It must have come slowly, this thing, I didn't realize anything was happening, I just knew my husband was losing patience with me. I'm constantly afraid, I've lost four stone in weight. I don't know why, but I think I've worried it away; when you are in a state of perpetual fear, it must do something to you mustn't it?

"As far as the future is concerned I just go from one day to the next, and try not to think about what may happen ... just as I don't make it happen. This fear that you've forgotten to do something gets hold of you and won't let you go. My husband and I have devised a checklist which we systematically go through before we can leave the house to go anywhere. It's a horrid feeling; I just only ever wanted to be happy and this thing just crept up on me. It didn't happen overnight, and now it's ruling my whole life.

"I used to be a happy little thing, but now I'm a mass of doubt and insecurity. I feel guilty but I don't know why, I just know it's all my fault ... it's my 'headbox' that's acting up, I'm causing distress to others; my husband has visibly aged 20 years in the last four years. But they don't understand it's out of my control; I'm not doing it on purpose. They get cross with me at times and lose their patience. If I was a four-year-old child, they wouldn't. But because I'm not, they do.

"Are there really others like me out there, or am I alone in this?"

As may be imagined, there are not many published accounts of what it is like to experience an appreciable severity of dementia. Maureen, with her as yet retained insight, is able to share with us the frustrations and worries of someone in the early stages of these difficulties; when it comes to more serious deterioration all that is possible is to make creative guesses about what the experience may be like. It has been likened to the sensation we all have when waking in a strange bed after travelling to an unfamiliar area. For an instant we wonder where we are. There are familiar objects around us: light fittings, furniture, the bed we are sleeping in. A room with a door. And yet while these are in a sense familiar in that we have seen similar objects before, they are nevertheless strange. Then, an instant or two later, all falls into place. Of course! We flew to France yesterday and this is our holiday hotel room. Dementia sufferers, perhaps, never achieve that 'of course!' realization.

The analogy of travelling in an unfamiliar country is a useful one. There is a great deal that is mysterious and confusing. As time goes by some well tried and repeatedly used routes, places and people become familiar and, like a toddler clinging to his mother, we are only fairly happy in these familiar surroundings. I remember, for example, my first visit to Russia. Our excursion coach stopped, unknowingly to me only because of a traffic signal, and precipitately I jumped off, to see it start off down the road again. I looked around me. With dismay I realized I had no idea where I was, had no map for clues (and, had I had one, all street names and signs were in an incomprehensible language and script). Worse, I hadn't a clue where I was staying: we had been taken to a hotel from the airport the previous day, a hotel in some anonymous suburb that looked ominously like every other suburb we had passed en route both the previous day and this. The name of the hotel eluded me — again, the Cyrillic script I could neither pronounce nor spell. People sped past me, marching with brisk purpose. Whose was a friendly face? If I sought help, could I make myself understood? What could I say beyond "I'm staying at a hotel 20 minutes away by coach somewhere on the outskirts of this city"? When I tried, I would be like that parody of an Englishman abroad who speaks not a word of the language and compensates by talking slowly and loudly, as if to a half-wit.

For me, this tale of woe had a happy ending: this book is not being written in a foreign land. Someone with dementia is not as fortunate. Apart from some basically familiar landmarks, most of life must seem foreign, confusing and frightening. Foreigners demand things of them which seem demands, and yet cannot be understood. What is understood is that the foreigners seem to get angry and impatient, and often to be shouting. Perhaps dementia sufferers get angry with themselves: for being unable to do what has previously been simple and taken for granted; for having things on the tip of the tongue, but being unable to get to the word or words they want to say; for being so forgetful; for losing control of what they want to do.

The issue of lost control may well be central to the experience of someone with dementia, control over both things around them (the washing machine and cooker, the car in the garage) and feelings and thoughts inside them (memory and understanding). In the early stages of a dementia people almost certainly have an awareness of their personal control breaking down in this way, and their seeming helplessness to regain it must be very frightening indeed. Added to this, they face the irritation that others show at their increasing helplessness.

Stroke

This is easier to identify with than dementia; there are enough people around to tell us what it is like. The actual stroke itself is rarely painful; in fact about a fifth of all strokes occur while the person is asleep. For those awake when the stroke occurs, about a third will lose consciousness, and about half will feel very confused or sleepy. Where the person has a degree of paralysis, it is common for the affected part of the body to feel very heavy. Trying to move at all involves great effort, and may lead to little actual effect. Any movement effected initially is clumsy and slow, with little strength. Where recovery takes place, the finer, skilled movements involving co-ordination (for example, the pincer grip of thumb and forefinger) are the last to return. The early weeks of this kind of paralysis can involve a cruel tease, in that certain involuntary reflex movements may occur in the affected limb, even when yawning, for example, giving rise to the hope that sensation and control are returning. While for many people this will happen, these reflex movements are just that — an automatic reflex action that occurs in the same way your leg twitches when the doctor taps your knee — and do not signify recovery. Moreover, with disuse, muscles develop a degree of stiffness or spasticity, which can be painful.

Stroke also commonly affects physical sensation and, although feeling is rarely lost completely, it is common for the affected side to be less sensitive to the nuances of texture. Frequently there is a degree of neglect of the affected side. At its simplest this can mean that the victim of the stroke stops trying to use the affected side of their body, and a common refrain from those involved in the rehabilitation of victims is to remind them to make every effort to employ the 'weak side' to the best of their abilities. In its more serious form this neglect can reach the point at which the stroke victim no longer recognizes the affected part as even belonging to them: it is someone else's arm or leg. To the stroke victim this phenomenon seems chiefly a source of irritation; to their loved one it can be quite frightening, and they may fear that the person is now going mad, to add to any physical effect the stroke had.

Stroke can affect that part of the brain involved in the planning of sequences of detailed movement. In practical terms this disability (technically referred to as apraxia) may mean that an activity such as getting dressed, having a bath or washing dishes becomes impossible, even when there is no 'paralysis' of a limb, and individual, constituent parts of these sequences of behaviour are possible, such as putting a pullover on or turning a tap. The ability to think through and plan the overall sequence is lost.

The ability to speak or understand speech is commonly affected by stroke. Communication is a very complex process, involving different areas of the brain. Depending on the location of brain damage, different aspects of expression and communication may be affected. The victim may talk in a confused and nonsensical way, even though individual words are articulate and clear. Or the victim may be quite clear thinking and know what they want to say but be quite unable to 'find' the words to express the thought. They may, however, be able to write the thought but not speak it, or conversely have lost the ability to express themselves in writing. Another problem that can develop is that of a difficulty controlling the muscles involved in speech, so the result is silence or slurred speech. The latter is very common indeed following stroke, and the person will say that their lips and tongue feel clumsy. They are only too aware that their speech also sounds clumsy. In contrast, the victim who has difficulty finding the right word to express the thought (dysphasia) may or may not recognize that problem, and persist in using a nonsensical word for an everyday object that makes perfect sense to them, and leads to frustration and irritation because it makes none to us. Indeed the dilemma of someone who is hospitalized after a sudden stroke which has left them without language has been compared to that of a person who is 'knocked unconscious during his regular daily walk, wakes up in a cell surrounded by captors who cannot tell him why he's there, who do not understand what he says, and who speak in a foreign language he doesn't understand'.

Vision is also commonly affected by stroke, and a bewildering variety of visual disabilities can result. One important problem is that of hemianopia, when half the visual field is lost; for the victim it is as if a curtain has been half drawn in front of them, and all vision lost to one side. The victim will be convinced that they can no longer see out of one eye, but in fact the area of the brain that sorts out the information from one 'side' of each eye is damaged, not an eye at all. In practical terms this may mean they ignore objects to one side of them and repeatedly bump into things. Not surprisingly, people with this condition are not allowed to drive. It is a very distressing condition that takes some learning to live with, and, curiously, people whose left visual field is lost seem worse affected than those who lose the right, finding it more difficult to learn to move their head to compensate.

Stroke victims commonly feel very emotional, being subject to bouts of tearfulness or anger. Aspects of this presumably relate to their distress at what has happened to them, but this does not seem to be the whole story. Victims feel somewhat out of control of their emotions, and this in itself can further fuel distress.

There are perhaps three main crisis points in respect of stroke:

1 The time of the stroke;
2 Discharge from hospital and the recognition that there may be long-term problems;
3 Final discharge from any out-patient treatment, for example, physiotherapy, and the realization that you are now 'on your own'.

At the time of the stroke, the victim is in a state of shock, and when this wears off there may be some over-optimism about complete recovery. In part this comes about because most of the recovery that does take place tends to do so early on, and also because, as noted above, certain reflex movements may convince the victim that movement is coming back to a lifeless limb. Unfortunately these over-optimistic feelings can be encouraged by well-meaning staff or friends and family, but in fairness to them it is difficult to maintain the right balance between realism and keeping an appropriate degree of hope alive. When unrealistic hopes do wear off, in situations where there is a degree of permanent disability remaining, the stroke victim can feel extremely cast down, usually after a period of feeling extremely angry at the unfairness of it all. This anger can be directed at anyone who gets in the way, and there is a tremendous sense of frustration and the invidious comparison between what was possible previously in life and now, with these disabilities. Stroke, unlike many other disabling conditions, gives little time to make this adjustment; the problem is there overnight, and the adjustment is made the more difficult by the uncertainty as to just how much recovery will take place. Because of the emotional flatness that develops, which can amount to frank depression, it can be difficult for the victim of a stroke to motivate themselves and develop as great a degree of independence and quality of life as is still possible.

As well as the suddenness of becoming disabled there is the sudden change of roles with family, friends and work colleagues. A capable, independent man who has always tended to take care of a rather nervous, shy wife, now finds himself depending on her, almost needing her to be nurse to him, or vice-versa.

Depression

It is still easier to put ourselves in the shoes of someone suffering from depression for two reasons. First, most of us make claim to some personal experience of what the feeling is like. In saying this, it is important to realize that there is a profound difference between being clinically depressed and being unhappy. When unhappy, even miserably unhappy, perhaps after suffering a major setback or misfortune, we are still 'reachable' in the sense of others offering comfort, sympathy and support. We retain the capacity both to be comforted and also perhaps to comfort others going through a bad time, and also can usually glimpse some 'light at the end of the tunnel' or recognize that this mood is unlikely to persist forever.

Some depression seems clear-cut and easy to understand, when it follows some major trauma, particularly of loss. We easily identify with the person who feels depressed following bereavement, or after learning of their terminal illness, or who can no longer speak clearly or walk following a stroke. Less easy to understand are those 'depressive personalities' who seem troubled by a lifelong tendency to depression, who seem demoralized by adversities or setbacks most would shrug off as part of the normal rhythm of life's ebb and flow. The depressive personality is usually tormented with low self-esteem and tends to feel both helpless and hopeless in the face of life, feeling that little is under their personal control. Those with depression see themselves as being far more inadequate and — importantly — powerless than in fact they are (although in saying this it must be pointed out that depression is a condition which does rob the sufferer of the energy and motivation most of us can take for granted).

Feeling inadequate and lacking a basic core feeling that, despite a few warts here and there, one is basically a reasonably worthwhile person, depressives are extraordinarily sensitive to the opinions of others about them, and concomitantly extraordinarily sensitive to criticism and personal rejection. (Because of this sensitivity to criticism and personal rejection, depressed people also tend to be extremely sensitive of other people's feelings, and tend to be over-deferential for fear of causing upset.) Some psychologists argue that this emotional sensitivity is caused by distortions in thinking, as when too quickly interpreting a friend's lateness for an appointment as evidence of no personal importance, where in contrast a non-depressed person kept waiting initially thinks non-rejective thoughts along the lines of "Bill's car's broken down" or "Bill's boss has kept him late again."

While research does seem able to identify these 'cognitive biases', it begs the question of how they arise. Clinical impression strongly suggests that depressive personalities come from unloving or fault-finding parental backgrounds. Loss figures highly in the background of people who are vulnerable to depression; this may be a loss in the sense of not having experienced, as a very young child, attentive and caring parents who delighted in their accomplishments, or loss in the sense of having lost such a parent through their death or parental separation. Infancy seems an extremely sensitive period in which to experience this parental interest, affection and delight in our accomplishments; without it one becomes akin to Henry's bucket: no matter how much one is loved later in life there is a hole in the psyche which makes a sense of one's personal worth well-nigh impossible to restore. Many of a depressed person's efforts are nevertheless directed towards an attempt at this, however, and these 'efforts' include their sensitivity to the feelings and sufferings of others. And these efforts have their cost. Feeling repeatedly criticized and rejected means that anger is never far beneath the surface, although this may very rarely be expressed.

Crippled with depression, the person travels weighed down by a sense of the injustice of the world, lacking any belief in themselves, save that all they attempt will fail. And there is a great sense of longing:

Thou art indeed just, Lord, if I contend
With thee; but, sir, so what I plead is just.
Why do sinners' ways prosper? and why must
Disappointment all I endeavour end?

Wert thou my enemy, O thou my friend,
How wouldst thou worse, I wonder, than thou dost
Defeat me, thwart me? Oh, the sots and thralls of lust
Do in spare hours more thrive than I that spend,

Sir, life upon thy cause. See, banks and brakes,
Now, leaved how thick! lacèd they are again
With fretty chervil, look, and fresh wind shakes

Them; birds, build—but not I build; no, but strain,
Time's eunuch, and not breed one work that wakes.
Mine, O thou lord of life, send my roots rain.

(Gerard Manley Hopkins)

People who are depressed also tend to cripple themselves with unattainable goals, their thoughts often being along the lines of "I must get everything I do perfectly right." Quite apart from the emotional misery this attitude inevitably brings, it also causes a kind of thinking overload. Overwhelmed with an enormous list of things 'needing to be done' (perfectly), they find it difficult to give conscious attention to any one of them, and this in turn can give the impression of poor memory as individual items are not attended to. When someone who is depressed is able to attend to some individual thing, this leads to an immediate, temporary lifting of spirits, perhaps almost to the point of exuberance for an hour or two as some of the (usually self-inflicted) load is lifted.

Common Threads

While victims of different disabling conditions experience widely different problems, to end this journey it is worth considering an area they share. This is the experience of a sense of loss. Amongst other things, perhaps including a particular technical skill, this loss may include some or all of the following:

- dignity and independence
- self-esteem and status
- recreational and social skills
- affectional and sexual expression
- confidence
- motivation
- job
- enjoyment of life

People are surprisingly resilient, and the majority of people with handicaps learn to live alongside them, albeit sometimes uneasily. In our efforts to help people with disabilities, as carers we very often get things wrong. But in their long and difficult journey, all that most victims ask, realizing that some of the problems they face cannot be cured, is that the other cares enough to try.

4

Coping Practically

ON BECOMING a carer, you need to find what services are potentially available to you in your area. These may be services in respect of assessment (establishing what is wrong), financial help, laundry assistance, volunteers to sit with the person you care for or day care facilities. There is likely to be a wide range, no matter how 'impoverished' your area seems to be in terms of cutbacks and so forth; the secret is in getting access to them. Be prepared to be systematic and persistent. One difficulty is that there is unlikely to be one resource centre or person with comprehensive knowledge of all that is available; if there is, you can thank your lucky stars and move six places forward immediately! Inevitably most people start with the family doctor, who may or may not have a wide knowledge. The doctor will know where to seek more specialized assessment of the medical condition (if necessary) and where you can get counselling. A library is a good port of call, and is always included when existing carers' groups advertise their existence. Some towns do have drop-in centres specifically geared towards the needs of the elderly.

Helpful Personnel

In your travels as a carer, you may come across a number of health care workers that come from professions you have not heard of before. The following is a reasonably exhaustive list of these professions, with a few notes as to the role they might have in respect of the kind of problems the person you care for has:

Consultant Physician

A consultant specializing in general physical health. A family doctor who is concerned, for example, about the possibility of dementia but wonders if ill-health may be causing confusion and forgetfulness may refer to this person for an expert opinion.

Geriatrician

This is a doctor (you are likely to see the consultant at least once) who specializes in physical problems in the elderly.

Psychogeriatrician

A doctor specializing in the mental health problems of the elderly. Having trained as a psychiatrist, they have specialist knowledge in psychiatry of the elderly. When the person you care for is elderly, the psychogeriatrician is an important specialist on many counts. First, they will have the expertise and experience to help clarify the picture diagnostically — you are likely to have a better idea of what is wrong with the person you care for after this consultation. Second, they have access to a wide variety of support services, both in terms of hospital beds and special units (for in patient and out-patient treatment and assessment) and of support personnel—other professions who will help with assessment, treatment and support. A referral here should help you feel taken under the wing of a range of supportive services.

Clinical Psychologist

In terms of numbers, clinical psychologists are quite thin on the ground, but you may come across one working in the NHS provision for the disability of the person you care for. They have expertise in connection with the assessment and treatment of a wide variety of psychological problems and will be able to offer you counselling as a carer. Clinical psychologists are trained to assess the nature of psychological and emotional difficulties that somebody may be experiencing, and are well used to treating not just the individual person who has the problem, but also advising others who have to live with it. They are not medical doctors, so will not prescribe medication, but rather concentrate instead on trying to find psychological solutions to the difficulties people face. They tend to be specialists, so are likely to have considerable expertise about the particular area of difficulty you are experiencing.

Social Worker

This is someone who is able to help you with a wide range of practical, financial and personal problems, and who often has considerable knowledge of services available in the area, for example respite care facilities and day centres run by the local authorities (as opposed to being a NHS facility). They may also know a great deal about what is going on in the community in the way of support groups.

Many carers are referred to a social worker early on in their contact with the health service (some social workers are attached to NHS facilities). If this does not happen and you are feeling particularly stressed, it may be worth asking if this can be arranged, as social workers are particularly well trained with respect to the strains carers experience in their day-to-day caring, and will help facilitate professional support to enable you to carry on at home, assuming that you wish to. They may be able to facilitate respite care and the appropriate financial benefits to ease this burden. It is usually a straightforward matter for them to visit you at home. (In fact most of the professionals listed here will be able to visit you at home, at least on the first occasion for an initial consultation.)

Physiotherapist

Physiotherapists have a role with people who have suffered a stroke and are left with a degree of weakness or paralysis. Physiotherapy aims to help the victim relearn use of the affected arm or leg, and provides exercises to combat the development of limb stiffness. Some movements are best avoided, as they encourage stiffness or other problems, and advice will be given about this, and how to regain balance, if lost, and general mobility skills. Where there is an appreciable degree of movement difficulty following stroke, physiotherapy advice is important. Stroke victims very typically 'ignore' or neglect their 'weak' side, concentrating on what is easy to do with the unaffected side. Although pragmatically this may seem to lead to the quickest progress, it does not facilitate long term recovery.

Physiotherapists can also help people suffering from Parkinson's Disease, and will give advice about ways to tackle walking difficulties. They are also an important source of advice about areas such as lifting a person and getting them in and out of the bath or bed. This is vital for *your* physical health.

Occupational Therapist

You are most likely to come into contact with an occupational therapist as a member of a team working in a day centre, day hospital or in-patient facility, although some are community-based and visit people at home.

Occupational therapists are trained in skills of assessment and assistance with problems in living with disabilities. They may do an assessment of daily problems, at a treatment centre, home or both, and have knowledge of a wide range of aids and strategies for helping overcome difficulty. Problems needing attention may include dressing difficulties, inability to get in and out of chairs, getting up the stairs and using cutlery or domestic equipment. Practical aids can help with some of these difficulties, as can learning new approaches to performing these skills.

A major role of this profession, as implied by its title, is helping people occupy themselves constructively and therapeutically. This means much more than keeping Richard busy all day; the therapist will encourage activities which keep him busy in ways which help with concentration, eye-hand co-ordination, balance, use of a partially disabled limb and so on; that is, practising the skills he *needs* to use. These may include socializing with others because of a tendency to withdraw into himself. They may include developing a new interest which can hold his attention and bring added quality to his life.

Continence Adviser

This is most usually a specialist nurse, often attached to a family doctor's surgery, who has had particular training to advise about incontinence. They have a good knowledge of the various aids that can be used, such as pads, penile sheaths and bags.

Speech and Language Therapist

This person is an important resource for someone with certain kinds of speech or language impairment. The therapist has specialist skills in assessing the nature of the impairment, and will advise about its management and the best use of any remaining language ability. They may offer help on an individual basis, or see the person you care for as part of a group of people suffering from similar difficulties, or perhaps use a combination of both. These therapists have expertise about aids to communication and may suggest these where appropriate. They are able to suggest the best way for people to talk to someone suffering from a particular communication disorder and ways to maximize confidence.

Speech and language therapy is a small profession; far more therapists are needed than are available. Consequently individual therapists tend to be overstretched and there may be some delay in seeing one.

Community Psychiatric Nurse

Community psychiatric nurses may be attached to a particular health service facility, for example a day hospital, but for the most part work out in the community, visiting patients and their relatives in their own home. They can offer emotional support to both patients and their carers, and help to give and monitor the effect of medication. They usually work closely with a consultant psychiatrist or psychogeriatrician and other members of a multidisciplinary team, and have an important role in co-ordinating this therapeutic input. They may, for example, alert the consultant to any deterioration or need for respite or permanent residential care, or the need for a further medical or psychological assessment. Part of this person's remit is continuing assessment as to whether the present level of professional support offered is adequate, a task which is facilitated by their access to families in their own home by regular visits.

Orthoptist

This is a specialist who assesses visual disabilities. It is not uncommon for people who have had a stroke to be left with problems connected with their eyesight, and this happens when the area of the brain which receives signals from the eyes (which are themselves unaffected) is damaged. An orthoptist can help with accurate diagnosis of the visual defect and advise the person themselves and those involved in their care about compensatory strategies and rehabilitation. Such advice might, for example, include suggestions about the positioning of objects and using special spectacles which move the visual field for those who cannot see half of it. They are able to write prescriptions for glasses and arrange for further treatment, such as ophthalmological assessment.

Others

In addition to these professionals employed by the statutory agencies, the NHS and social services, there are numerous people in the voluntary sector and charitable organizations that may be of help to you. The Stroke Association, for example, trains support workers to visit and assist people who have suffered a stroke in their own homes. These people often become very experienced and knowledgeable, and the support they offer can be invaluable. Similarly the charity Crossroads offers support to carers, and some branches have experienced volunteers available to offer a 'sitting' and befriending service. Charities such as Age Concern and the Alzheimer's Disease Society can offer expertise and advice, and publish a wide range of helpful literature.

Your Health

As a carer, you do no favours to anyone if you let your health break down, and this is an area that needs equal consideration to that accorded to the person you care for. This includes taking sensible precautions to safeguard your health, eating properly and seeking medical help for yourself when appropriate.

Caring for a person disabled by stroke or dementia may well include a good deal of lifting, for example, assistance with dressing and bathing or toileting. If it does, the effect is cumulative, and if lifting is done incorrectly this will lead to chronic back pain and possibly other problems. Accordingly this must be thought about, and each major lift planned and executed with care. Some principles of lifting are given here, but ideally these should be demonstrated by a physiotherapist.

In general:

1 Before starting any lift, plan it and get into position.
2 Stand with your feet apart, as close to the person you are lifting as possible.
3 Keep your back straight (but not stiff) and bend at your knees and hips. Keep elbows as close to the body as possible.
4 Tense your stomach muscles and make the muscles of your legs, particularly the thighs, do the work.
5 Do not twist your body during the lift.

As can be seen, this does require thought and planning, at least until it has become second nature. Be especially careful if you are tired or feeling stressed, at which times you might grow careless and injure yourself. There may be aids which could help you, such as a hoist.

While it may seem laughable to talk about exercise, this is perhaps an area to think about. Even where caring does involve a great deal of physical exertion, this tends to be of a particular kind, for example repeated lifting, washing or dressing. This is not the kind of exercise that tends to leave you feeling invigorated and cheerful, and it is worth considering whether some *enjoyable* physical activity could not become a regular part of your life. The emphasis on enjoyment is important: you have enough chores in your life already without adding to them. And, particularly when your caring does not, in fact, involve that much physical exertion, the tiredness you feel most of the time is likely to arise from the way you feel emotionally. Here you will be surprised at how much livelier you feel after exercise. To introduce into your life some pleasant activity that involves exercise will benefit your health and give you something of an emotional lift; we all tend to feel more positively about things after exercise that is interesting, whether it is a walk in the park, a game of tennis, a swim in the local pool or whatever else it might be.

Breaks and Respite Care

An essential part of looking after your health and that of the person you are looking after is to ensure that you have some time to yourself, for you to use as you please, even if this is only 30 minutes in a hot bath with a pot of tea and a magazine and the door locked. Part of your weekly timetable must include a day or two when you can have several hours pursuing your own interests or meeting friends. If this seems impossible, sit down and work out why. Sometimes, particularly if they are caring for a husband or wife, people feel guilty about going out or doing something by themselves — almost feeling they are being unfaithful, or selfish, not sufficiently caring. Yet no-one would expect a car to run forever without periodic maintenance and regular fill-ups with petrol. You cannot care indefinitely without also accepting care for yourself from time to time. This has nothing to do with selfishness or being 'not good enough'. Quite commonly, having felt guilty about wanting more time to yourself, you may find yourself feeling angry with the person you care for — why can't they see you need more of a break? — and this anger in turn makes you feel even more guilty. If these feelings are getting in the way of your having some life to yourself, they need to be talked through with someone.

You may feel that 30 minutes in the bath is not possible because the person you care for follows you everywhere and will not let you out of their sight. There are many tales of carers who feel obliged to let the person they care for into the toilet while they perform! We will look at this problem, with a suggestion or two, later, but if you find no solution to it, this is a sign that you need some kind of respite care. This might involve a friend or someone else in the family well known to the person you care for (who can manage his epileptic fits or other problems) who will 'sit' for an hour or two and let you get your hair done or go for a walk around the block. Another way is to make use of a day care centre run for elderly people by the NHS or social services or, for example, 'stroke clubs' where someone who has had a stroke can go once a week. This is an area your doctor will advise you about.

Part of pacing yourself and avoiding exhaustion is learning to make priorities. If you get the person you care for into a day centre where they are cared for one day a week, this is *not* a good opportunity to catch up on housework; it *is* a good opportunity for you to meet a friend, see a film, write to Aunty Mary in Australia who was so fond of you all those years ago. Your health is more important than the house being as clean as it was before the person you now care for became ill; a little dirt never hurt anyone, it builds up resistance!

This time to yourself, for yourself (and others, such as children) must become a regular part of your week. Try asking friends and family to offer a sitting service. They will need to be informed about the condition of the person you care for, and you will need to stay the first few times to be sure they are confident, so that you can leave with peace of mind. It also makes sense to build up the time this person is left alone with the 'sitter' little by little, so they get used to your increasing absence. But be firm about this, as long as the person doing the sitting is happy for you to be so (one sign of a good sitter who is coping is one who pushes you out of the door and tells you to be firm). Some branches of Crossroads offer a sitting service and this may be available from the statutory agencies.

In addition to this, it is very often appropriate to negotiate for regular respite care, whereby you can make use of a residential setting for a week or two every six weeks or so. Your family doctor or other concerned professional will know what suitable facilities are available. This kind of arrangement can be a godsend, transforming what had become an intolerable grind into a manageable proposition, with a fortnight's relative freedom to look forward to on a predictable basis. Respite care will give you a chance to recharge your batteries and live to fight another day, and is something that all carers looking after someone with severe disabilities owe themselves. The obstacles to achieving this are very often emotional ones, with the carer feeling too guilty about accepting this service something we will look at in Chapter 5.

Minimizing Risk in the Home

This is an area about which there has to be a sense of compromise; you are not going to be able to eliminate all risks, no matter how conscientious you are, and accidents happen even in the best run hospitals, but you will be able to sleep more easily and leave your dependant in order to go out for an afternoon more happily if you give some thought to minimizing some of the bigger hazards. People with intellectual impairments involving memory and concentration are of course more vulnerable to accidents: they may forget pans on the stove, leave newspapers dangerously near gas fires, forget the proper dose of an essential medicine or forget to take it at all; they may forget about the pothole in the back garden path "we all know about and avoid". Please do spend an hour or two going around the house, room by room, to assess these kind of risks, perhaps adopting the frame of mind you have to in caring for an active toddler; this is not treating the person you care for as a toddler, but rather reminding yourself of the dangers when other people do not have our mindfulness of risks. Although you will want always to have some awareness of it, having done this exercise you should not let it become an obsessional preoccupation.

Financial Help

One major and very practical problem facing many carers is financial hardship. Caring full-time for a disabled person is an extremely costly business. Some costs are quite apparent, such as extra laundry bills, heating and clothing; others are less immediately obvious, such as the inability to work yourself in paid employment. There are a number of Social Security allowances with the express purpose of helping to ease the burden. Information about these benefits and allowances tends to date quickly, and accordingly no specific details are given here. However, your local Department of Social Security office or the Carer's National Association should be able to give you up-to-date advice.

Some of these allowances can prove difficult to obtain when there is a dispute about the degree of disability. Should this situation arise, the first step is to send off an application form (available from the local Social Security office), after which a doctor will be sent out to make an assessment of the amount of help the person you care for needs. Where there are clear physical difficulties, such as those following a stroke, this is often clear-cut; but in other conditions, for example, dementia, the degree of disability may be less immediately apparent. If the person you care for has an unusually good day on the occasion of the assessing doctor's visit, this may give a misleading impression of the severity of the difficulties generally facing you. For this reason it is a good idea to give the doctor a previously prepared written synopsis of the problems this person has and how much practical help (for example, with dressing and toileting) you need to give.

Many people are diffident about accepting this kind of help (it is known that fewer people claim benefits than those who are entitled to them). The reasons for this are many and often complicated. But you have a right to financial help; the reality is that the government saves a great deal of money by your caring. You must be prepared to be persistent, and may need to apply more than once. First applications can be rejected, only to succeed on appeal, and there seems to be some variation in the way different local Social Security offices deal with similar disability and caring needs.

There is a free and confidential telephone helpline on 0800 666555 which will advise about benefits, but the people at the end of it will not be able to deal with a claim. For this, and for detailed up-to-date advice, approach your local Social Security office, the Citizens' Advice Bureau, or your social worker if you have one.

For those caring for someone with dementia, the Alzheimer's Disease Society has a 'Caring Fund' available to supplement statutory allowances for those still facing severe financial hardship after receiving their entitlements. There are three categories for which carers can make an application:

1 Equipment and improvement of the home (one-off items).
2 Necessary travel and crisis care (this might include carers in urgent need of a break).
3 Miscellaneous items, such as having a telephone installed, heating bills or car tax.

Financial Provision for the Future

When caring for someone, bear in mind the possibility that you may not always be able to manage them at home, and that at some stage they may have to go into a residential facility. There will be assistance with this for those unable to pay for it, but it is means-tested and dependent on the amount of savings you have. There are companies which offer insurance to cover the eventuality of needing residential care, and which will then pay the fees, but, as you would expect, at a hefty price. The premiums depend, reasonably enough, on age and level of cover required, and there are companies offering to pay annual fees of a residential or nursing home for a lump sum. This is business, and each case will be looked at individually; for an older, frail person you would pay a small lump sum, not surprisingly. These schemes may be worth some thought.

Legal Arrangements

Where the person you care for is severely intellectually impaired, or likely to become so, it will be necessary to think about this area, for example in respect of your finances now and in the future. This will be particularly so if your house is in your spouse's name or jointly owned and there is a chance that you may want to sell it, or in respect of money that may be in this person's name. It may be appropriate for you to secure a 'power of attorney', which gives you a legal entitlement to manage another's affairs. This can simply be given by one person to another, but the arranging solicitor will want to be satisfied that the person giving this 'power' is mentally capable. As by definition this will often *not* be the case (unless you and the person you now care for have been able to plan ahead), transfer of entitlement can only be effected by application to the Court of Protection. Where you and your still capable partner are able to plan ahead, you will need to arrange for an 'enduring power of attorney', which does not lapse in the event of intellectual deterioration. Needless to say, this is a delicate area. If discussing it with a person who is perhaps, say, in the early stages of dementia causes a great deal of animosity, it is probably better to leave it for the time being, although later application to the Court of Protection is a rather formal and complicated procedure. The Court will appoint a receiver, who might be a solicitor or member of the family, to manage a mentally impaired person's affairs. A fee, based on the latter's income, is charged for this, and it can be an expensive business. Fairly simple matters like the paying of bills and collecting pensions and other benefits are not too much of a problem and, to collect a pension on behalf of someone else, all that is necessary is to become an 'appointee' which can be arranged by the local Social Security office. The Court of Protection provides helpful free leaflets about enduring powers of attorney and the Court of Protection in respect of the estates of people suffering from mental disability; the address is given in Appendix I. Mind Publications also publish a book about the workings of the Court of Protection; details are given in Appendix II.

Professional legal advice can be expensive, but if finances are limited you may be entitled to free or subsidized legal aid. The local branch of a Citizens' Advice Bureau will be able to advise about this, and may themselves offer a free legal advisory service.

5

Coping Emotionally

GETTING ORGANIZED practically will be an important step on the road to coping emotionally, but we need here to look quite specifically at the emotional side of things. Carers are vulnerable to depression themselves, and this may lack the attention it needs in its own right, preoccupied as you and others are about the needs of another person. There are a number of issues to consider.

Having Sufficient Practical Support

The importance of sufficient respite care has already been stressed, and this is a key area in terms of the carer's emotional well-being. In addition to this, do explore what other practical support may be available to you, such as a laundry service, sitting service and home help. Do other members of your family help out? We consider this below.

Having Sufficient Emotional Support

Some of the feelings that carers have to face are explored in Chapter 7. These range from initial disbelief and anger on hearing the news of their family member's condition, to grief, guilt, hopelessness and lethargy. The first thing to recognize is that these feelings are quite normal (it would be a little surprising if you had none of them) and need expression. People vary in the way they handle distressing feelings. Some wear their heart on their sleeve, pouring everything out to anyone patient enough to listen. Others keep a tight rein on their feelings, weeping alone, if at all. Most, I suppose, steer a middle course, sharing feelings only with a trusted friend. While it is often unwise to generalize, there is some evidence to suggest that simply bottling up feelings of distress and never expressing them leads to trouble — for the one who bottles them up. This trouble may take different forms, perhaps a variety of physical problems, as the feelings come out in that way as aches and pains, or, possibly worse, as some kind of breakdown. Shakespeare, who knew most things about human nature, spoke of this too, in *Macbeth*:

> Give sorrow words; the grief that does not speak,
> Whispers the o'er-fraught heart, and bids it break.

and in *King Lear*:

> The grief hath craz'd my wits.

Having sufficient emotional support means having someone you can talk to who will keep quiet and listen—listen to you ranting and raving, listen to you weeping. If you hear, "Pull yourself together", find a different listener. As in all spheres, the best listeners are 'wounded healers', people who have experienced the same things for themselves. Here is Shakespeare again, in *Much Ado About Nothing*:

> . . . everyone can master a grief but he that has it.

So getting together with others in the same boat can really help, although you should make sure that some of your companions have learned a few tricks of the trade in managing, and that it is not just a complaining session which lowers everyone's morale. Ask professionals involved with the person you are caring for if there is a carers' group you can join. If there is not, prod them into starting one. Local societies for the problem you are facing (such as Alzheimer's) often exist, and can be found through the local library, local hospital or social services department. They are a good starting point. If they do not exist, maybe it needs you to make them happen. Useful addresses and telephone numbers are given in Appendix I.

Ideally, of course, you will be able to share things with members of your family, but this is often easier said than done, for many reasons. Not all families are emotionally close by any means, and you may never have been able to share frustration and distress with them, or a spouse, and receive a sympathetic response. If this is the case, trying to do so now will only fuel your distress and, realistically, you will have to look elsewhere for this support. In the final analysis, this might be someone professionally involved, such as a social worker, community psychiatric nurse or clinical psychologist.

Families can only support you emotionally if they know how you are suffering. Some carers become a martyr to the cause, feeling they have to do everything. Here the rest of the family's unwillingness to do anything may be as much in the imagination of the carer as within reality. Another common difficulty that carers face is other members of the family not seeing just how difficult the person needing care can be ("Richard's all right when we visit"). This problem, too, can exist for a variety of reasons. To your frustrated disbelief, Richard may be better on the occasion of a visit from relatives. Depressed people, for example, are commonly able to conceal their sadness behind a facade of normality for short periods, and someone even severely demented may brighten up considerably and respond in quite a lively way, say, when grandchildren visit, when for all of the previous day carers in both of these situations were able to get not a single word out of the person they are caring for. Other family members may also see Richard as 'not being that bad' because they need to, as a way of coping with their guilt about not helping more.

It is not at all uncommon for one member of the family (often the only daughter) to somehow end up taking sole responsibility for caring for a disabled parent. Although it makes practical sense to be living in one place, try to get other members of the family to share as much of this burden as is feasible. This may necessitate some kind of quite 'formal' family meeting the formality of which can be used for you factually to relate all the difficulties you face as principal care giver. Another powerful way for the rest of the family to come to appreciate this is for the person you care for to spend a week with them!

Do bear in mind that both friends and members of the family may be reticent about offering help because of their feeling helpless and uncertain about what they can do to help in the situation. This feeling of impotence is common among friends and relatives of someone who has been bereaved, and can lead to what is experienced as an avoidance of them. You may be able to help them to help you by being explicit about what they can do: sit with the person for an hour or two to give you a break for a bit of shopping or whatever. In doing this, try to use whatever talents they have anyway; a sister known for her extraordinary patience might be the best choice to sit with and amuse a person who says the same thing over and over again; the friend who jumps at any excuse to do a bit of window shopping might do some shopping for you, ideally taking the person you care for along at the same time!

Setting Realistic Standards for Caring

A very common theme when I listen to carers is that of guilt. This comes up in a variety of contexts: feeling guilty that a moment's lack of supervision led to a fall or burn, guilt when Richard looks so miserable when the ambulance collects him for respite care; guilty about complaining about Richard when carers in the carers' group have more disabled Richards, guilt about the times you have shouted, the times he got a slap. . .

A wise child doctor and psychoanalyst, Donald Winnicott, wrote a great deal about a mother's care for her baby. Whilst enormously moved by the care given by the 'ordinarily devoted mother', he wrote without sentimentality about this, saying that a parent's care need only be good enough. There were broad limits to this care; obviously it could be so bad as to be inadequate, but equally perfection, even assuming it could be attained, would serve the child no favours either, in that such a child would grow up quite intolerant of frustration. There is a message here for us. Your caring for Richard needs only to be good enough, and there are times when some carers need to remind themselves of this and try just that little bit less hard. Striving for perfection the whole time will exhaust you quickly and probably lead to some kind of breakdown in your own health. To state the obvious, this does neither you nor the person you care for any favours.

A good example of unrealistically high standards getting in the way is seen in the context of the carer's acceptance of respite care. Many carers feel guilty about this, even when they themselves are exhausted. They feel particularly guilty when the person they care for makes it plain that they are unhappy about going away from home. The first time is almost inevitably difficult, with a renewed surge of guilt, to the point that they may be unable to use the break. They may feel so unsettled ("Will the staff cope; will he be really miserable?") that it is no holiday for them at all. They may then feel the experience was so stressful for them that it was counter-productive and decide never to do it again.

This first-time experience for carers is so common that it is perhaps universal. If you can go into the exercise knowing that you are highly likely to have these feelings it will help you through the first time. Things do improve. Those of you with children may well remember a first day at school, nursery or playgroup when your child was highly distressed. You were torn in half on leaving, and spent a miserable day with a picture inside your head of your child crying all day long. Anxiously you went to collect them at the end of the day, to be greeted by cheerful staff who said that the child settled as soon as you were out of sight — and indeed there she was playing happily with others, not even noticing your arrival! The scenario is often equally true of respite care, and Richard will eventually settle and get used to the arrangement if you stick to your guns and have regular respite breaks.

Some people make caring a crusade or mission, becoming a slave to it. In fact it can become someone's whole existence, to the point that, when the person they are caring for dies, the carer feels they have no other life at all. You owe it to your own emotional and physical health to have a part of your life apart, wherein you grow yourself. Although realistically interests and hobbies that you may have will go by the board for a time after the onset of caring, do not let this inevitable early state of affairs continue indefinitely. If you have never had much in the way of an interest, now is the time to start, crazy as this sounds. Take up pottery, painting, music — something to use the creative part of yourself (we all have a creative part). Nurture this in the same way that you look after the person you care for. Then there is also a life after caring.

You may rest assured that professional care, either in the National Health Service or in local authority/social service provision, is based on an acceptable compromise of 'good enough' caring. The word 'compromise' here is significant: you are unlikely to be professionally trained as a carer, unlikely to be an expert on specific disabilities, likely to have a heavy burden of other responsibilities, likely to have finite financial resources and likely to have limited practical support. These are all factors which necessitate some sense of balance as to the standard of care you can give. That you have turned to a book like this suggests a level of concern which in turn suggests you are not a carer who will set this standard too low.

How Realistic is it Emotionally for You to be Caring for this Person?

Many books for carers have a phrase like 'caring for someone you love' in them. Uncomplicated love is rare, and indeed it may be that now you are in the position of caring for someone with whom you have had a difficult relationship over the years. This situation can be extremely stressful. Your reasons for caring at all in this situation may be quite complex, varying from a sense of duty to arising in part from a sense of reparation, making right now what could not be made right before; and in part they can come from a sense of guilt. Caring for a parent you have never got on with is particularly painful, reawakening distress that goes back a lifetime. Perversely your spouse in this situation may not see what all the fuss is about — they have always thought Richard was a 'decent sort of chap' and cannot understand the fuss you are making. They do not realize that your annoyance now with your father or mother arises out of a hurt that is deep in the bones from years ago, and that you castigate yourself for being unable to 'live and let live'. Part of the difficulty of this situation is that when caring is compensatory and driven by a sense of guilt and wanting to make reparation, a sense of persecution develops and very strong feelings of anger are rarely far below the surface. Initially, and perhaps most often, this anger is directed at yourself — for not caring better and making it all fine — but on occasion too it will spill out towards the person you care for, family, friends or anyone who gets in the way at the wrong moment.

This all needs very careful thought. There is a difference between the periodic feelings of irritation and anger common to most caring situations and an awareness of a deep anger that is there most of the time, fuelled by a corrosive resentment that this person never cared very much for you before they became ill. If you sense that this kind of resentment is the case for you, it is a wise step to talk this through with one of the professionals involved, taking care to say at the outset that you need some counselling about this area, so the appropriate person can be selected. They will help you come to a decision about how realistic it is for *you* to continue caring for this person at home.

Recognizing that Feelings are Getting out of Control

There are times when any long-term carer looking after a person with major difficulties will feel unappreciated, angry, depressed and simply worn out. It is not at all uncommon for carers to have feelings of wanting the end to come, half hoping the person they care for will pass away in the night. This is a perfectly normal feeling, but carers may feel appalled at themselves for having such thoughts, seeing themselves as some kind of monster because the thought has even entered their head. So, as well as feeling unappreciated, angry and exhausted, a carer is often further burdened by a sense of guilt caused by the thoughts that all these other feelings lead to.

But, again, there is a difference between having these feelings and thoughts from time to time, even quite frequently, and being overwhelmed by them all of the time. It is not unusual for people in your situation to become very depressed and reach breaking point. You may have feelings of extreme anger and find yourself being verbally or physically aggressive to the person you are caring for and then be overwhelmed with shame and still more guilt. Caring for a severely disabled person is not easy and there are few saints living in this world (those few that are about are impossible to live with!). Quite apart from characteristics of saintliness that may or may not be present, the fact of the matter is that a high proportion of carers are themselves no longer young, and often in poor health as well. If you are overburdened with distressing or frightening feelings, do recognize that this may be a sign that you need help, and do not feel embarrassed about talking to your family doctor and asking for it. If necessary make it plain just how desperate you have been feeling, and ask for a suitable referral to someone experienced in counselling carers. They will not be shocked by what you have to say.

Coping: a Summary of Principles

1 Organize.
2 Prioritize; do not fight unnecessary battles.
3 Do tackle treatable problems that cause stress.
4 Care for your own health; provide for adequate rest, both as a regular part of the week when you have time for yourself and, when appropriate, as respite breaks of a week or more every so often. Try to have some enjoyable exercise as a regular part of your life.
5 Care for your emotional health. Do not sit on angry or depressed feelings; find a friend or counsellor you can talk to.
6 Accept all the help you can; be explicit to friends, family and members of the statutory authorities about what would help you.
7 Claim all financial entitlements.
8 Have a life apart from caring: time for friendship and interests.
9 Remember that caring has to be good enough, not perfect.
10 Recognize when caring at home is impossible.

6

Practical Problems

First Principles

As a first step in considering how to deal with some of the usual problems carers face, let us take some advice from a little girl called Christine:

> Dear Grandma I know its hard for you when Grandad says you bugger larua and thorws a spoon at you. but its not his folt or when he lights his sigaret the wrong end he just foregets things but anyhow hes still a good Grandad you'll have to discurrge him not to thorw spoons at you if you don't want him to thorw a spoon at you. Hes all ways nice to use but never you I do not know way but thats the way it is and I know how you feel but we can't change the way Grandad is because hes lost his trolly when he throrws a spoon at you. but lets not talk about Grandad anymore. Thank you for the money. I don't know what to by its going to ither be a

carcot, Babybath, baby clauses, or a high chair or a pair of slip on shoes for me. Anyway you don't want to know about that or I might put it in Barcley Bank. I don't want to leave you. Know I love you both you know just because hes diffrent in some ways and your kind.
Love
> from
> CHRISTINE   XXX

p.s. Please can you do a family tree. I wood be very greatfull. Hope I see you at Christmas.

Christine knows about an important psychological strategy, 'reframing', and the wisdom of a healthy dose of distraction!

We will look at a variety of problems the person you care for may have, such as sleeplessness, confusion about what time of the day or night it is or about people (not recognizing you, for example), memory problems, apathy and lack of motivation, clinging, dependent behaviour, sexual difficulties, incontinence, aggression and marked personality change. We will also include your practical problems: dealing with all of the foregoing, not being able to have time to yourself, embarrassment with friends, social isolation and exhaustion.

Given that caring is something you may be doing for many years, it pays to organize. A regular timetable, day by day, will help you to pace yourself and so not get overtired, and will also help reduce any confusion in the person you care for by providing a sense of routine and consistency. Further to these advantages, if you talk to an actor they will tell you that, regardless of how they had been feeling previously, they feel sad after acting a tragic part, happy after taking part in a comedy. Feelings can in a very real way follow behaviour — what we do. Accordingly having a sense of being organized and on top of things will go some considerable way towards helping you cope at an emotional level.

In this chapter we will look at some problems faced by some carers. The list is not exhaustive, nor is it a list of the problems all carers are likely to face. Specific suggestions will be made as to how to try tackling some of the more common difficulties. Before moving on to particular problem areas, however, it is worth reviewing some general principles to be observed when approaching any area of difficulty with the person you care for.

Dignity

In trying to put ourselves into the shoes of this person, the overwhelming experience is seen to be that of loss. A major part of this loss is dignity. It is not very dignified to be unable to control your emotions, thoughts, memories, speech, limbs, bowels or bladder.

Dignity is probably one of the most fundamental of human rights. It may be easy to lose sight of this when faced with incontinence for the sixth time in a day, ten minutes after suggesting going to the toilet, to no avail, and with five sets of soiled clothes in the wash. But shouting at the person you care for will only make them feel worse and you feel guilty, and it will not do the laundry or help you see what can be done. Although this principle holds true for any stage of a person's illness or disability, nowhere is it truer than in the early stages when they have insight into their lack of control and themselves feel humiliated by it.

Avoiding Confrontation

During a war, some battles are not worth the cost of fighting — the war can be won without them. This is true also of caring. Do not make an issue out of a problem for the sake of it. In dementia, sufferers tend to stick to the well-tried and familiar, hating intensely any change. So they may become passionately attached to one or two shirts, dresses or a coat, and always want to wear them. This is sad to see, particularly in a person who previously had a strong sense of pride in their dress. But is it worth the battle to get them to wear something else? The battle will exhaust you and them, and prevent either of you enjoying the afternoon out.

Remember that this person *is* disabled, and you have to avoid putting unreasonable pressure on them. Someone who is depressed cannot 'snap out of it': if they could they would do so gladly; being depressed is hardly a bundle of laughs. Equally it is pointless constantly to correct a person with dementia who says something 'absurd', such as calling you 'mother' when in fact you are their wife. This would include the person who (clinging to what little remains of their dignity) insists that you have stolen their purse when they cannot remember where they put it; or who says you spilt tea over them and they have not wet themselves again. Confrontation in these situations makes people face their lapses of behaviour and, where this might be appropriate with someone in perfectly good health, it is essentially cruel in a situation of genuine disability. Being forced by this kind of confrontation to face difficulties is a not uncommon trigger of aggression in dementia. Yes, it is always easier to give three pennyworth of good advice than to be in the situation yourself and take it, but the reality is that you will make life easier for yourself and the person you care for if you keep a tight handle on confrontation.

Encouraging Independence

Some years ago, a piece of research which looked at the skills retained by people with dementia in residential settings was carried out. The research team expected to find a range of skills, varying from reasonable competence to complete dependence. In fact they found a 'bipolar' distribution of skills: in general residents either could exercise a particular skill, such as dressing or washing, or they could not, and had to have assistance with all stages of these. This was a worrying finding, because in general terms you would expect to find a range of skills, with, for example, groups of people needing no help, a little help, quite a lot of help to absolute assistance.

The tempting conclusion is that, in many situations where people with disabilities are seen to start having difficulties, the carers take over and do the job for them. This is understandable; it is a seeming kindness and often a lot quicker. But, and here's the but; this is not the way to preserve abilities for as long as possible. Skills eroded in this way, through well-meaning kindness or impatience to get the job done as quickly as possible, very rapidly disappear through disuse. Then you have a person who really cannot do very much for themselves, and you have this distressing situation sooner than need be. Certainly you can do it more quickly, and of course it is difficult to see someone struggling with something they would have done in a flash without thinking years ago, but as a general guiding principle it is of the utmost importance to let people do what they *can* do.

Be generous with your praise (obviously without being patronizing) when the person you care for demonstrates their independence and has a go at something for themselves; this might be a decision to do a mundane chore by someone depressed, or an attempt to button a cardigan by someone with dementia or by someone who has lost the use of one arm following a stroke. Obviously this will mean that you have to be prepared to adjust your previously held expectations about standards of acceptable daily behaviour, modifying them in the light of the present disability of the person you care for. Where a particular activity is clearly beyond the person's capabilities, a significant degree of independence is retained if they have a go at one of the constituent components of the overall activity, for example putting the cardigan on but leaving the impossible buttons to you. This is important for this person's morale, as much as anything else.

Minimizing Stress

It is obviously impossible to eliminate all stress from the life of the person you care for, but a little thought will go some way to minimize avoidable crises. This might include, for example, leaving you both plenty of time when going to an appointment or shopping (allow double the time you think you will need!) and discouraging too many relations visiting at the same time. You should also avoid turning yourself into a hermit.

Do try to keep as much of your home life as usual as is possible. Again this is easier said than done, but keeping as much of your previous life intact as possible will not only be a comfort to the person for whom you are caring but also reduce the impact of loss on you.

Adapting

A well-known joke involves a bottle with wine halfway up it, of which the pessimist says it is half-empty and the optimist that it is half-full. It is an unfortunate human characteristic to emphasize disability: what is not there, what is difficult. In all of the conditions considered by this book that carers attend to and care for, there is a great deal that is missing, wrong and depressing. But to survive you must try to rejoice in what is still there, and what can be achieved together: the smiles; the times you sit in the park together; the excitement when the grandchildren visit. Some of these things will even be new—like finding out just how good and decent, how patient and caring *you* can be.

To adapt means to accept it when the person you care for finds it easier to use fingers or a spoon to eat; to accept it when they reject the new pair of trousers you bought them; to accept your sadness; to accept your pleasure at finding the depth of kindness inside you.

Typical Problems

We will now look at some particular problems that some of you may face in caring for the person who depends on you (we will call him Richard). This cannot be an exhaustive list and the suggestions made are tentative. One of the best ways of finding solutions is to chat to others in the same boat to see what works for them.

With any problem, it is essential to become something of a scientist or explorer to solve it. The first step is easy, because you do nothing—except keep a diary to make a note of:

- **when** the problem occurs (for example, 8am and 10am on Wednesdays and Thursdays);
- **where** it occurs (for example, every room in the house, but never outside or in Betty's house);
- **what was happening** before the problem occurred (for example, I was leaving the lounge to go to the kitchen);
- **what happened** after the problem occurred (for example, I lost my temper).

If you keep a careful diary of a worrying problem in this way for, say, a week, you often detect patterns you might not otherwise have suspected. An example might be that Richard only follows you when he is doing nothing. Noting a pattern like this is the first step towards finding a solution: for example, in this situation, making sure he has a magazine or some photographs to look at when you desperately need some space. This exercise, even if it does not lead to you finding a solution, will be of immense help to others, should you need professional advice.

The problems may seem endless. Again it pays to make priorities and tackle only the unbearable problems; some battles are not worth the cost of fighting. In any event, tackle one problem at a time. Decide, for example, to make a concentrated effort at finding something which still amuses and interests Richard for a few weeks, rather than trying simultaneously to reduce his confusion, tackle his forgetfulness and work on incontinence.

Once you have your diary record of the problem, try one technique to deal with it and continue the diary for another week. Is there any change in frequency? If not, try another idea. If you try several things at once you will not know what works, and you will get discouraged if, unknowingly, you stop practising the effective technique and go back to square one. This is not easy and demands patience, but when it works the rewards are worth the time spent. What immediately follows a problem can profoundly influence the problem occurring in the first place, which is why with your diary record it is important also to note these 'consequences', and perhaps systematically to try changing them. To give an illustration of this in practice, you may note from a diary record that saying "You *are* at home" in reply to someone with severe confusion and memory failings as part of a dementia process has no impact at all on the frequency with which they repeat, "I want to go home." However, the diary also shows that responding to these statements by sharing memories with the person of the life they had in the area where they lived previously does help.

Forgetfulness

Typically in dementia it is recent memory that is most severely impaired. Thus someone may forget what you have said five minutes ago, but remember details of their childhood. Although they may have *immediate* memory, in that they can repeat back what you say, the breakdown occurs in them putting this information into a more permanent memory, so they cannot 'hold' it for five minutes, still less a day or two. Their capacity to add to long-term memory is damaged.

The repeated questioning from someone with memory impairment, particularly when it is the same question you have answered many times already, is intensely irritating. It may even seem on occasion that this is being done deliberately just to annoy you, but in reality it happens because the person has not only forgotten the answer, they have forgotten they have even asked the question before. Looking at it from their point of view, to be shouted at when they ask meekly when someone is visiting, not realizing they have asked 10 times in the last half an hour, must seem a bit unreasonable!

Unfortunately, when memory is impaired by damage to an area of the brain, it is impossible to restore to normal as one would, for example, strengthen a torn or injured muscle with exercise. This does not mean that nothing can be done, but rather that we are looking at palliative aids to make the most efficient use of what memory remains. To return to the analogy of the injured muscle, we have to accept that in the case of memory, the 'leg' will never be as strong as it was before the accident, and instead we have to provide a crutch to maximize its remaining strength.

Most of us use 'external aids' to memory to act as cues in our daily life—the knot in the handkerchief, the shopping list, the book with telephone numbers. With someone with memory difficulties, these aids need to be made as specific and helpful as possible; the knot in the handkerchief reminds us we have to remember something, and our memory is normally good enough with that simple cue to bring the specific event to mind. It may not be with Richard. Equally a reminder as you leave Richard for two hours to 'turn the gas off when you have finished with the soup' is unlikely to be remembered when he is actually cooking lunch some hours later. Cues work best when they are:

1 *Active*: someone saying something or seeing a notice that cannot be missed, or a bell ringing.
2 *Relevant or specific*: a list stating what items to buy or a notice spelling out what needs to be done —'buy a present for Jill's birthday which is tomorrow, 15 September'.
3 *Given in close time and place proximity*: a reminder just before something needs to be done, as opposed to hours earlier; or a notice in the appropriate context, such as 'Have you washed your hands?' hung by the toilet door so it is seen on the way out.

Indifferent or poor cues, which might still be good enough for us but which are likely only to lead to failure and frustration with the person with poor memory are:

1 *Passive*: an entry in a diary with no other active cue to remind them actually to look in the diary.
2 *Non-specific*: a note saying simply, 'Jill's birthday'.
3 *Distant in place and time from context*: saying, "Have you washed your hands?" after Richard has come downstairs from the bathroom.

So, for example, if Richard forgets he has left something on the cooker, we might teach him to set an alarm clock for an appropriate interval each time he puts the cooker on. If he keeps the clock with him, the alarm might remind him of the cooker, particularly if there is a small card with 'COOKER' written on it (or a picture of one if he cannot understand written language) placed by the clock.

Richard's forgetting which is his bedroom, or the way to the toilet (which can be a contributory factor in toileting difficulties) can be helped with a particular colour for the door of these rooms (and a small card in his pocket with these colours and appropriate pictures as well, perhaps). If that is insufficient, try a coloured ribbon stuck to the wall or floor that can be followed as a map, and a picture of a bed or toilet glued to the appropriate door.

Those who are less disabled may be able (perhaps with help with the programming) to use an alarm digital watch and a daily diary, with the day's necessary events programmed at the start, each hourly alarm acting as a cue to look in the diary for the next event. They are likely to need some training to use this system.

With all confused memory-impaired adults, it can be helpful to have a large notice-board in the main living room (the kind you write on with felt pens and which can be wiped clean), listing which day it is and important events for the day ('Jill coming with the children at about 3 pm'). Ensure that clocks, calendars and dates are accurate. Someone who can read may well be able to cope with tasks they have 'forgotten' how to do if you write out instructions. If you are going out, write on the notice board where you are going, what time you will be back and a reminder to eat or use the bathroom if appropriate. If Richard has difficulty with written notes, instructions can be given in pictorial form. Always read out such reminders as well, for spoken material is better remembered than written, and best of all is to use both together. Also try to make Richard need to think about the item to be remembered, by, for example, talking about things associated with it, as this helps memory. So with repeated questions from him such as "When is Jill coming?", rather than simply saying, "Three o'clock" 20 times (and getting exasperated in the process), try "Three o'clock; do you remember, she usually comes just before we have tea on a Saturday", and then get him to talk about his associations with Jill and teatime.

With a person in the early stages of dementia, memory impairment may be quite minor, and in fact not at all obvious to others. The person may have an awareness of their own problem, and be at some pains to hide it, perhaps getting angry, seemingly for no reason, when this is in some way exposed. Strategies of the kind suggested will very often help, but only if everyone concerned, and that includes you as a carer, feels comfortable about their use. Sometimes carers can resent the house being 'cluttered' with notice-boards, or drawers and cupboards having labels pinned all over them; and the person cared for may resent what can feel like being treated as a child. You can be sure that if there is this kind of resentment around, the strategies employed are unlikely to be very effective. A man paralysed by an accident and who remains angry indefinitely with his wheelchair collects many grazed knuckles as he tries to propel himself furiously through narrow doorways, and moreover makes less speed than his more accepting friend.

Even when someone's memory is clearly poor, in the sense of their being unable to remember things verbally, do not be defeatist and see this as a sign that their memory is hopeless, full stop. People with very clear impediment in their verbal memory often show appreciably better recall when they are able to demonstrate this by their actual behaviour, for example learning a new route to a particular room or a new jigsaw. Having said this, a memory is often context related, and lost (sometimes usefully so) outside that context. A good example of this is seen when we stay in a hotel on holiday. We very quickly learn and remember the number of our hotel room, only to forget it soon after coming home. This has particular implications where there is an appreciable degree of intellectual impairment, as in dementia, where learning and memory may be particularly context-dependent. A skill most of us can take for granted, continence, may be quite precarious in someone with dementia and thus highly dependent on context, and may be lost in a move to new surroundings, whether a residential home or a relative's house on the occasion of a fleeting visit.

A mention needs to be made here about the effect of someone who is hard of hearing. It has been known for some time that people with appreciable hearing loss seem to have poor memory. This is not simply because they do not hear, and therefore obviously cannot remember what has not been heard in the first place, but rather it is true for what they *do* hear. What seems to happen is that people who are slightly deaf have to concentrate so hard on catching what is being said that they do not have the time at normal conversational speeds to think also about the contextual *meaning* of what is being said. Consequently a common complaint made by the hard of hearing is that other people 'mumble', and do not make much sense. Those of us without any impediment to our hearing are able to concentrate on meaning quite automatically, almost without any conscious thought, and an important benefit by way of side-effect from this is to lay down a stronger memory. If the person you care for is hard of hearing, please bear this in mind, and be careful to speak clearly and perhaps also to slow your normal conversational speed slightly, allowing plenty of pauses. You will need to exercise care about this so that it does not come across as patronizing and indicating that you have decided that Richard is half-witted!

Thinking generally about forgetfulness, routine, although it may make life seem a little regimented, can do a great deal to make things easier. Confusion and memory impairment are intermingled in dementia and can combine, with large swings of mood. Richard may become highly distressed over what is seemingly a trivial matter, such as where he left his newspaper, particularly if he has a degree of insight into his memory loss. Dementing people can easily become overwhelmed by aspects of daily experience we take for granted, such as an unexpected visitor. Having previously enjoyed reading the daily paper, someone with dementia can be left with some ability to read, but little ability to understand the meaning of the words or text. Reading the paper then becomes exasperating precipitating a seemingly inexplicable outburst of temper. If this happens, try to remain calm, if necessary taking Richard to a quiet place away from a cause of distress (if one is obvious). Touch is reassuring to most people, although not to all and may be misinterpreted as aggressive by someone with dementia. Argument will almost certainly make things worse. Shout at a pillow in your bedroom later! Returning for a moment to the problem of repeated questioning, write the answer down on the notice-board in your living room, simply point to it the next time the question is asked and try drawing Richard away to some other focus of attention.

Confusion and forgetfulness about who you and other family members are are common. This can be both difficult and quite painful to deal with if, for example, Richard mistakes you for his father, who died 30 years ago. It does not seem to matter how many times you tell him, it does not sink in. When you or your relatives have time, Richard can often be reorientated (even if only for those few minutes) by spending time going through photographs of you together, reminiscing. It is, alas, much more difficult for someone with severe memory impairment to come to terms with a bereavement; they will keep forgetting that they *are* bereaved. In dementia, as the years go by, the person will become increasingly less aware of later life experience, for example a bereavement they experienced in their early sixties — hence the commonly heard statement of relatives or a spouse: "They remember everything of their childhood quite clearly, it's the recent past that's gone."

When the person you care for does get confused about people, it can help to become something of an imaginative detective rather than repeatedly correcting them (which is unlikely to have any corrective effect anyway). So if Richard asks what time his father, who died 30 years ago, is coming today, and in fact your daughter *is* coming about four that afternoon, it is a reasonable supposition that it is the situation of a visit from *someone* that day that is around in his mind and you can respond to that. So you reply, "Our daughter Jill is coming about four. That's when she usually comes on Sunday. Let's hope her car doesn't let her down like it did when they went on holiday"—rather than telling him yet again about his father.

Where there is memory impairment, try to encourage Richard to be systematic about things: his glasses always go on the table by the fireplace, his wallet always goes in that drawer in the sideboard. Although there are differing opinions about this, in my view it is also a good idea for someone with severe memory impairment and confusion who may wander off alone to have some means of identification, such as an identity bracelet which includes their home address, to help should they get lost.

Difficulty in Performing Simple Daily Activities

Simple tasks can seem or actually be impossibly difficult for someone suffering from dementia or the aftermath of a severe stroke. They may have forgotten *how* to brush their teeth. People who have suffered a severe stroke can be left with visual problems or disabilities of movement which make this kind of task particularly difficult. The occupational therapy department at a local hospital may have helpful advice about techniques and aids which ease everyday household jobs. One trick is to try reteaching the task by breaking it down into small parts, for example, starting with teaching how to hold a toothbrush. Sometimes slowness in doing something is mistaken for an inability to do it. Taking over at this stage means the slow person will lose the abilities they have, impaired though these may be. This may require you to accept lower standards than you would ordinarily be comfortable with (for example, as regards the tidiness of Richard's clothing), and this will be difficult for you. But you may find it is a price worth paying, both for the morale of the person you care for and for easing the burden on you.

Clinging, Following and Wandering

Richard's being always one step behind you and following you from room to room can be intensely irritating. This may happen in a person with damaged memory who cannot remember that you always come back from the kitchen. For a confused person you are the only source of security and consistency, and they will cling to you in the way a toddler does to his mother. Emotional insecurity is very often a central issue in this. Taking people with Alzheimer's Disease, there very often comes a time when they come to believe that their long since deceased parents are still alive, asking when they will next see them and when they will be 'going home'. Given that suffering from dementia and being unable to rely on your intellect and previous skills is likely to feel frightening, the dependant searches for reliable and familiar parental figures who will make them feel safe as their mother made them feel safe as an infant. This emotional need for the parent comes on top of a substantial memory impairment (forgetting that both parents died years ago), with a resulting extremely strong conviction that one or both parents are alive, confirming the availability of the comforting familiarity and safety of the childhood home. This conviction is resistant to any amount of reasoned argument, and in fact anything which leads to anxiety in the person you care for, such as tension in the house or strangers visiting to fix the television, will fuel this search for past security, to the point that some people will actually set off for their old home of 60 years ago. This emotional dilemma is never actually resolved, alas, save in the sense of their attachment and clinging to you, often, indeed, to the point where you *are* Mum or Dad.

Although Richard's wandering around the house may seem quite aimless, this behaviour usually has one of four main underlying causes:

1 A search for emotional security—looking for you/Mum—as described above.
2 Confusion about *where* they are (as may arise, for instance, following a recent change of house or from memory failings).
3 Influence of previous work roles (such as house work or DIY); thus the man who used to work shifts gets the household up 'as usual' at 4am!
4 A life-long habit of coping with stress (for example, restlessness or going for a walk).

In addition to these possible causes, bear in mind that the person may simply be physically uncomfortable!

Thinking about Richard's restlessness within this

framework may suggest some ideas to try. Taking his need for emotional security, providing him with a cassette recording of you talking over old times (or singing away in the bath!) and some photos of you or the family may help him better tolerate your going into other rooms without him. Boredom may well be a factor. Does he always sit in the same chair, looking at the television he cannot really understand? Can he see through an interesting window? Helping him find some interest he can enjoy (if only sorting through a button box or old photos) will reap benefits. Someone who has always been active may pace round through physical frustration. Exercise is particularly important here. Maybe a friend or neighbour could take Richard along when they walk the dog? Whether or not these ideas prove helpful, if the problem in this area is severe, look at the possibility of some 'sitting service'.

Night-time wandering is looked at in the following section.

Insomnia

If insomnia troubles you as well as the person you care for, you may both benefit from this section.

The frequent, immediate solution that is often used out of convenience is sleeping medication. This is effective in getting people off to sleep, though not so good at keeping them asleep (early waking is common). Quality of sleep tends to be poor, and people tend to need an increasing dose of medication as the body gets used to it. Such medication has its place, particularly if things have reached an intolerable pitch, but try to see its use very much in terms of a short-term crutch; certainly not as a method to rely on for more than a few weeks.

In general terms, it is important to establish healthy routines to promote sleep. Exercise (not last thing at night) and a degree of pleasant recreational interest during the day (as opposed to napping on and off throughout for reasons of boredom) are important. For those with sleep problems it is unwise to develop or continue with habits such as reading or watching television in bed. As part of the evening routine, aim for something gently relaxing before bed, a bath perhaps; watching the news with horrific pictures from a war-torn country last thing at night helps no-one to get to sleep; watch the news earlier. A light snack including carbohydrates with a warm milky drink (not coffee or cocoa) before retiring helps. It may well pay to reduce caffeine intake generally: less tea, coffee and fizzy drinks; in particular do not consume any drinks containing caffeine during the evening. Research has shown that as few as four daily cups of coffee can increase the time taken to get off to sleep, and also reduce the amount of actual sleep time by almost half an hour. People also become more sensitive to the stimulating effect of caffeine as they get older. Some folk swear by herbal remedies; I recommend lime flowers tea.

Lack of physical exercise can contribute to the problem of insomnia, although exercise taken in the evening or last thing before retiring may well be counter-productive and be more arousing than inducive of sleep. Certainly, if Richard is napping on and off during the day, this may make him less likely to sleep most of the night. Frequent daytime napping can be a sign of boredom; it may be an effect of tranquillizing medication the person is on to control their behaviour. Discuss this with the doctor; it may be possible to achieve the same behavioural control by administering the medicine in the evening instead of the morning.

Elderly confused people can become particularly restless at night, sometimes getting up out of bed and walking around in what seems an aimless fashion. Research has shown that this is often caused by darkness and the disorientation that can then occur because elderly confused people are less able than ourselves to retain a 'map inside their head' of their surroundings. Waking in the dark disorientated means they become anxious and look for familiar landmarks. Being anxious, they may also look for reassuring company. A night-light bright enough to show familiar features of the room may help with this. Also it is a good idea to have thick curtains to reduce any traffic noise and shadows caused by street lights. Have a clock clearly visible at night from the bed. A light left on outside the bedroom may help reduce confusion. If Richard does tend to walk around, ensure the house is secure so that you can go to bed with peace of mind.

Thinking particularly of you the carer now, and problems you may have in getting off to sleep, a common refrain is that by the time you get to bed you are so tired that, cruelly, sleep eludes you. Or, preoccupied with problems, your mind races away, and again sleep takes hours to come. There are a couple of techniques to try, and in this it is assumed that you have already attended to all of the above that is relevant to you. First, get out of bed and write down your concerns or 'things you must remember to do' on a piece of paper, and if you think of a few more 10 minutes later, do the same again. This is so you are not lying in bed with your mind struggling with things you have to remember — not a good recipe for sleep. Second, make up your own nonsense word — 'glig' or some such — and repeat it over and over to your self non-rhythmically. Or, if you prefer, try counting one to 10 to yourself with a steadily shifting pause in the sequence:

one (pause) two three four five six seven eight nine ten
one two (pause) three four five six seven eight nine ten
one two three (pause) four five six seven eight nine ten

and so on, over and over. The idea behind this technique is to be doing something so easy as to be possible almost without attention and to be in itself quite hypnotic, but which also imposes just enough of a load on your consciousness to make you unable to direct thought to other, perhaps worrying, matters. At the same time, this imposed 'thinking load' is insufficiently demanding to keep you awake.

Hearing Hurtful Things and Facing Aggression

Being told that you do not care can be really difficult to cope with, when you patently do care and, moreover, are giving a great deal of your life to do so. Unfortunately, taking someone with dementia, the deterioration in the brain sometimes affects that part involved with the control over personal and social behaviour, which can mean that a previously polite person who was endlessly patient even when provoked now swears or lashes out over some trivial irritation. This deterioration to the brain also leads to a loss of social awareness; the person affected becomes largely unaware of the nuances of another's feelings, so that, for example, they have no idea of the effect their shouting has on you.

Looking at physical or verbal aggression from dependants with dementia, experience suggests a number of typical triggers and likely causes:

1 Impaired judgement means that someone with dementia may lose the ability to evaluate the seriousness of a given situation, so an otherwise trivial incident, such as your spilling some of your tea, is seen as a major catastrophe.
2 Loss of intellectual and social skills can cause a serious misperception of another's actions, so that, for example, removing a handbag to free a person's hands so they can eat more easily is seen as your stealing the handbag.
3 Being overloaded intellectually with too many questions or problems at once.
4 Being overloaded with unfamiliarity, such as an unexpected, unfamiliar visitor, or being in noisy, crowded and therefore 'unpredictable' places.
5 Being with someone who is feeling tense or irritable.
6 Being unable to complete a task that was once easy.
7 Being confronted with the carer's reality: "You *are* at home" or "You've *had* your lunch."

Thinking about all of these, some ideas about trying to manage, and preferably prevent, episodes of anger suggest themselves:

1. Try as far as possible to bring a sense of routine and predictability to the life of someone with dementia.
2. Within reason, try to make activities attempted by Richard failure-free; do not, for example, give him a cup of tea and a plate to hold; one will end up on the floor.
3. Simplify what Richard has to think about at any one given time by, for example, asking one question which lends itself to a simple answer ("Would you like a cup of tea or a cup of coffee?") rather than inviting endless rumination ("What would you like to drink?").
4. Explain what you are doing and why: "I'm taking your newspaper so you can hold your cup."
5. Ensure that other members of the family and regular visitors understand common areas of friction or particular triggers.
6. Give instructions about a particular activity that needs to be done one step at a time; if you want Richard to get dressed, and this tends to cause ructions, take him through it piecemeal: "Put your vest over your head; yes, that's right; now pull it down" — and so on.

When we are faced by someone who is angry, the instinctive reaction is to be angry back. In this context (if not others), this most probably makes things worse and leaves you feeling guilty. There is much to be said for counting to 10, leaving the room and coming back when things (not least yourself) have calmed down. This gives you a chance to channel your anger to where it belongs, that is to Richard's illness rather than at Richard himself. It can really hurt if you take remarks like "I want to go home" (when Richard lives with you) and "You have stolen my purse" at face value. Try to see what might lie beneath them, for example, "I want to go back to where I lived with my wife, back to when I was healthy and not a burden to anyone", and "It can't be that my memory is so bad I can't remember where I have put my purse, so someone must have stolen it." Putting this kind of distance between you and the remark is essential.

This is one situation where Richard's forgetfulness can be a blessing; in five minutes he will have forgotten what he was furious about. Again a diary record may produce a pattern of aggressive outbursts, which may give clues as to how to pre-empt them (such as finding a different way of asking for something or doing something at a different time). Anger may arise from Richard's confusion. He may misinterpret what is happening, for example, a child crying might make him furious, not with the child, but because he thinks someone is attacking or upsetting the child. Some people with dementia have visual agnosia, an inability to recognize objects or people by sight. Regrettably this may include you, a husband or wife of many years. Anger can arise when Richard thinks it is a stranger helping him undress or go to the toilet. The reassurance of your voice, saying who you are and what you are doing, will help to remind him.

All of us become embarrassed and uncomfortable when we lose our dignity in some situation, and the person you care for is no exception. Being confrontational with someone who has wet or soiled themselves, who has made a mess eating, who cannot remember where they have put their glasses, or who asks you for the twentieth time this morning what time the grandchildren are coming may make you feel better for a second or two, but it is also a not uncommon trigger for aggression, particularly from a person who retains a degree of insight into their disabilities.

If, after thinking about all of the points made above you remain seriously concerned or are becoming frightened, get professional help. A clinical psychologist may help to assess problems and find ways to ease things, a doctor might prescribe sedation (for Richard!). Aggression that is sometimes seen in dementia invariably mellows with the passage of time.

Incontinence and Toileting Difficulties

Of all the problems which you, the carer, have to deal with, a problem with toileting could be the one that comes to dominate the way you feel about the job. Coping with this undoubtedly places a great burden on carers. Double incontinence, of urine and faeces, causes the greatest burden of all. Perhaps what is more upsetting than the problem itself is the way in which the person for whom you are caring responds to what is happening. Some elderly confused people may lose the sense of what is acceptable behaviour and will often do things that will disgust their carers. Others will try to 'cover up' accidents, perhaps hiding soiled underclothes in drawers and cupboards. It is only natural for you to feel angry about what may often be perceived as deliberate soiling. Many carers admit to feeling revulsion and often to being physically sick when faced with having to clean up urine or faeces. Do not be ashamed of such feelings; they are perfectly natural. Remember that the person for whom you are caring may feel equally, if not more, disgusted than you about something over which they have no control. Talking to others, particularly other carers, may help you to see the problem in a different light. Some find it helps to see themselves as a nurse who would perform such tasks as part of their job.

No matter how hopeless things may seem, do not become too despondent—there is help available. It might also be worth while taking a few minutes to consider how you could help yourself. Continence involves a complex chain of behaviours:

1 Recognizing the need to urinate or defecate.
2 Selecting the right place for elimination and being able to get there.
3 Undressing.
4 Performing and practising hygiene.
5 Dressing.

A break at any part in this chain will result in toileting difficulties. An example of this is seen with the person who recognizes the need to urinate, but whose damaged memory makes it difficult to find the toilet and whose damaged language makes it impossible to ask where it is. Another such case is the man who recognizes the need to go, can find the toilet, but cannot unbutton his trousers.

It is important to make sure that the broken link is correctly identified, as each problem requires a quite different solution. If there is more than one broken link, this will be a little more difficult, but do try to channel any anger you feel into finding the broken link and exploring the possibility of doing something about it. You may succeed in a situation you had thought hopeless; if you fail you have the satisfaction of knowing that no stone has been left unturned.

The first step is to arrange for the person for whom you are caring to be medically assessed. Problems can result from certain treatable medical conditions, for example an infection, or, surprisingly, constipation (which can be masked by overflow leakage and soiling/diarrhoea). These are not infrequent causes of incontinence. Similarly some medicines can affect bladder control.

Next, take a moment or two to think about your home. Could the layout of furniture or rooms be contributing to the problem? Try sitting in the favourite chair of the person you care for and think about the route to the toilet. Is it an obstacle course for someone who is frail or disabled? Can they remember the way to the toilet? (Perhaps for Richard it is still at the bottom of the garden as it was when he was a child.) Is the bathroom warm, well lit and comfortable? Can Richard manage his clothing?

The following is a list of possible problems (broken links in the chain of continence) and suggestions for tackling them.

1 *No recognition of need to urinate.* An enuresis alarm (available through health clinics or family doctors) may, in the absence of marked brain damage, develop Richard's awareness of a full bladder.

2 *Urinating/defecating in inappropriate places, such as a corner of a room.* This shows recognition of the need to perform, and an ability to manage clothing. This problem sometimes results from the disorientation which can arise from a recent move of residence or even a 'simple' redecoration of the house. Encourage regular toileting in the toilet which has the door clearly identified by a particular colour (perhaps with a picture of a toilet on it) and ribbon of same colour along the floor from Richard's bed or usual chair to the toilet. Each time you toilet Richard, remind him you are following the 'blue ribbon to the blue door which is the toilet'. Praise success lavishly. Praising good behaviour is a far more potent method of encouraging change than punishing bad behaviour.

Poor eyesight can be a factor, and any elderly person should have regular eyesight assessments. Inappropriate defecation and urination sometimes occurs because of memory deficits — forgetting the appropriate facility for performing, and low motivation may arise particularly if the toilet is difficult to find, or Richard feels shabbily dressed anyway, or the bathroom is uncomfortable and cold. If Richard is unsteady on his feet, fitting bars to the side of the toilet will give added comfort and security to his visits there.

3 *Cannot manage clothing.* Dress the person you are looking after in clothing that will cause minimum difficulty and delay: dresses and skirts with a wrap-over opening at the back are useful for women; loose-fitting trousers with elasticated waists or a side opening and velcro flies can alleviate some of the

difficulties for men. Do not underestimate the psychological significance of attractive, comfortable clothing which with a little thought can also be practical. Leaving the person all day in pyjamas may make toileting easier but may also make them feel that they cannot be trusted. The resulting feeling of hopelessness may diminish their chances of regaining continence.

Often more than a degree of habit retraining is necessary. Here, as with other difficulties, it is essential to begin by making an assessment, this time by keeping a toilet chart. This will enable you to establish the times when urination typically occurs. Check as tactfully and sensitively as possible every two hours or so to see whether the person you care for is wet, and prompt them to go to the toilet. Record the information in a chart similar to the following:

		8am	10am	12noon	2pm	4pm	6pm
CONDITION?	WET	X	X				X
	DRY			X	X	X	
USED TOILET?	YES			X	X		
	NO	X	X			X	X

If, after a few days, you find that wetting or soiling follows a regular pattern, you can proceed with 'habit retraining'. This simply involves prompting toilet use some time, say 30 minutes to one hour, before the times recorded as WET, that is, in our example, 7 am, 9 am and 5 pm and at the times that they made use of the toilet. Visits to the toilet at other times can now be stopped.

It may be possible in some circumstances, to re-establish independent toileting. One way in which this may be encouraged is by offering rewards if they are dry. The 'reward' need only be your attention and praise. If they make use of the toilet when prompted, praise them again. If you find them wet, try to behave in a matter-of-fact way so that they can learn to distinguish between 'rewarding' and 'non-rewarding' behaviour. (You might find other, more tangible, rewards more useful.) Less disabled people may be reminded to take themselves to the toilet by an alarm clock ringing at appropriate intervals.

The above are suggestions worth trying. Sometimes, however, there may be such a degree of deterioration in the brain that you have limited success. Communication may be proving increasingly difficult and this can add to the problem. They may have expressive language problems which means they no longer have access to the right words to let you know they need to 'go'. Try to respond to what you feel they are saying. This will always be easier if you have kept a toilet chart as you will then have some idea of the times they are likely to need the toilet. Some may find having a picture of a toilet pasted to a card that can be shown when the need arises gives a way of communicating.

If memory seems to be a problem, they will need to be accompanied to the toilet and guided through the necessary sequence of events. Speak clearly and slowly while you do this, explaining each stage in turn. Always follow the same sequence, and, as far as possible, use the same words and phrases each time. Keeping it simple in this way will help the process of relearning.

Incontinence is a wearying, miserable problem. This is why so much space has been given to this topic. Research shows that it is a major reason for carers finally asking for residential care to be provided. Sometimes, though, a bit of a rethink about the situation and careful assessment and trying of particular ideas do lead, if not to a cure, to substantial improvement. If you have no success, be prepared to ask for help. Your family doctor or local hospital may be able to refer you to an incontinence adviser who can offer help with alarms, pads and other aids. Some local authorities offer a laundry service. Talking to others may show that many are in the same boat and will help to dispel what is for us a major taboo.

Sexual Problems

One problem that *sometimes* becomes very difficult for carers is that of the sexual relationship with the person they care for. Please note that the word *sometimes* is emphasized for good reason: not all carers will face difficulties in this area, and if you do not have any problems here you can skip this section.

Despite our culture's obsession with sex, when it comes to being able to talk about this aspect in the context of their overall predicament, carers may feel that they have been abandoned in an arctic wasteland. There is a remarkably powerful taboo about discussing sexual relationships in the area of disability, illness and older people, and this may be one of the respects in which carers come to feel particularly isolated. This is a good example of a situation where a supportive carers' group can help, making it possible to share frustrations and disappointments with others who are prepared to listen and, moreover, who have often experienced the same problems themselves.

There are many areas of potential difficulty in the sexual relationship between a carer and the person for whom they are caring. If this person has a condition that changes them out of all recognition, having sex with them might be tantamount to 'making love with a stranger', as one carer put it. This might be fine in the land of secret fantasies, but, as with most fantasies, it rarely works very well in practice! In the realm of fantasy, a partner is likely to be dashing and charming, attractive and vivacious, wanting us and us alone. If the person being cared for confuses the carer with their mother or father, has spent a large part of the day soiling their clothes and has been repeatedly rude for good measure, this is not a recipe for the most romantic of bedtime encounters! Nor is it the greatest of boosts to our ego when someone we live with (who is perhaps depressed) completely loses interest in sex, perhaps seeming to have expectations of us as a housekeeper alone. How do you make love with someone about whom you have entertained thoughts of murder all day? Or when you are simply so exhausted with the burden of caring you are not in the least interested? And to these variations add the nuance of an emotional truism: both caring and being cared for can reduce sexual desire.

It has to be said that there are no easy answers to such problems. Nevertheless we can look in some detail at a number of the common dilemmas and see if there are at least some strategies which will help.

When the person you care for is your spouse or partner
Continuing sexual intimacy between a carer and a disabled partner can be a source of conflict in many ways, such as the following:

1 The carer wants this side of the relationship to continue but the partner is uninterested.
2 The carer does not want to continue sexual relations ("It would be like making love to a stranger") but the partner does.
3 In principle the carer would like to continue sexual relations but is simply too exhausted by the end of the day.
4 In principle both the carer and the partner would like to continue a sexual relationship, but there are physical problems resulting from the disability that make this difficult.
5 Both carer and partner are uninterested (perhaps saying, "We're too old for all that anyway").

In the last situation, where there is congruence, stress in this area will be low, provided of course that this truly is the situation; in which case you are unlikely to be reading this section anyway. In considering the other situations, a good starting-point is to acknowledge that both carers and their partners have sexual needs and feelings. Change to a previously unchanging and long-lasting sexual relationship is a potent cause of stress and requires a process of readjustment.

The first three situations in the above oversimplified list are further complicated by gender. A male carer who wants sexual intimacy to continue may well feel that he is 'taking advantage' of a female partner who, if severely demented, may in a sense be said to be non-consenting. He may feel that his actions toward her amount to little more than rape. A carer of either sex who finds it difficult to feel sexual about their partner may find their thoughts turning to the possibility of sexual relief in other relationships. Whatever one's views are about the morality of this, feelings of guilt are common, and may be particularly acute when the other person is making overt accusations of infidelity anyway. Carers who still desire sexual intimacy and have difficulties of the kind referred to may be embarrassed to raise these issues for fear of being seen as exploitative, selfish or immoral. Other carers are unlikely to be judgemental; a professional counsellor will certainly not be.

Female carers may find it easier to tolerate the ending of sexual relations with the partner than their male counterparts; but even if there is some truth in this debatable assertion, it does not make this simply 'all right' for them.

Ordinarily, when a couple have sexual difficulties, a first step in counselling treatment is to facilitate communication between the partners, encouraging them to talk together openly about their problems and preferences. A counsellor would certainly want to see them together. Having clarified the problem, for example fatigue, anxiety about 'performance' or tension, the counsellor would suggest targets and exercises aimed at overcoming these. Where the emotional side of the relationship is good, the outcome of this kind of sexual counselling is often very satisfying for both partners. It is in fact one of those areas of psychological treatment that clearly 'works' in the sense that a problem can be cured. Where your partner has a disability that leaves reasoning intact, therefore, this professional help should most definitely be an option explored if an initial attempt to sort things out by yourself fails.

Usually, most couples will have a go at resolving things by themselves, and there are in fact a number of self-help measures worth pursuing. These include trying to discuss calmly how things have gone wrong and when they went wrong; the effect these difficulties are having on each of you; what—if any—aspects of your relationship together have led to these problems, and what steps can be taken to try and improve things. As an example of this, if a degree of emotional staleness or stress has been instrumental in sexual disenchantment or difficulty, you may agree together to leave sexual relations for the time being, concentrating purely on rebuilding emotional intimacy first.

When your partner's intellect is intact but it is impossible to resolve problems through discussion perhaps because of lack of 'motivation' or complete apathy and/or loss of libido, as in depression, it is important to treat the condition (depression) as a first step, and indeed this may prove to be the only action required, as other problems will often correct themselves as the depression lifts.

Where your partner's intellect is severely impaired, as in dementia, the normal process of sexual counselling is clearly inappropriate in that it simply is not feasible, particularly in the latter stages of the disease, to include your partner in the necessary discussion. With disorientation and memory impairment, someone with dementia is unable to think about the nuances of the relationship and learn new strategies for coping with their spouse's feelings. They may, for example, simply forget about the importance of the emotional and physical preliminaries to love-making. They may simply lose interest and no longer respond to your overtures. Emotional intimacy is very typically lost as a dementia process becomes severe. To state the obvious, this emotional intimacy is seen by most people as a prerequisite for sexual relations. In this situation we have to look at any strategies which may help the carer to cope.

An important theme of this book is that, to survive, a carer needs some emotional 'distance' so as to be able to see aspects of the other person's behaviour as the illness talking, rather than that of the person themselves. Nowhere is this need greater than with respect to the sexual side of their relationship, where there are difficulties. A person with Alzheimer's Disease may lose the capacity to be attentive and considerate, becoming instead demanding and perhaps physically aggressive; they may confuse the spouse with their parent; they may be sexually demanding and then forget that intercourse has happened immediately afterwards; they may say something hurtful during intercourse without any insight into the effect that this has. In all these cases, the carer must endeavour to see this behaviour as part of the illness and not as personal vilification, 'use' or rejection.

Another aid to survival is recognizing that sexually demanding behaviour may be a plea for reassurance about personal worth, attractiveness to the spouse and 'loveability'. It may be possible, in terms either of your own sexual needs when caring for a uninterested partner, or of helping a sexually demanding partner when you yourself do not feel so inclined, to translate sexual activity into other ways of expressing physical and emotional intimacy. A touch or hug may do wonders. In offering this suggestion, it is recognized that it will not always do so, and may in fact instead be construed as a sign of sexual availability and, if this in turn is not there, may be experienced as a tease — either for you or for the other person. You will have to exercise judgement about this.

A person who retains an interest in sexual relations with their carer may be unaware of the stress the carer is under and consequently of the carer's reduced interest in sex. Someone in the advanced stages of dementia may have little, if any, insight into how unreasonable, not to say off-putting, their behaviour may be on occasions: for example, staring with blank incomprehension or not even noticing, when the carer screams with pain after an accident in the home; being unaware of the impact that making sexual overtures has on a carer who has spent most of the day spitting murder; or being unaware of the effect of making advances to someone whose name they simply cannot remember, and whom they often confuse with a parent anyway. Unfortunately, without this insight, a person whose advances are ignored may feel hurt and rejected, not to say confused, if these advances were welcomed in days gone by. Why the change? They do not understand and, because of their condition, it is not possible to explain. Despite this, there are a number of strategies worth trying.

Talking to a friend or another carer may help you come to feel differently about the situation. It may ease feelings of guilt that are troubling you, and provides a safe outlet for you to ventilate anger. I have been struck by the humour in most of the carers groups I have attended; very often an individual member will be pulling their hair out about one of the painful situations discussed above, and yet after some thirty minutes they are laughing uproariously with the others. Yes, as our mothers always told us, laughter is a great healer.

It is always worth trying to talk to the person you care for; never assume this is a waste of time. If however you find that this not only leads to no change but also increases your distress, clearly it is pointless.

Talking to a counsellor or one of the professionals involved with the person you care for, for example the social worker or psychiatric community nurse may well open up new ways of thinking about the situation.

Try taking more of the initiative. Before their condition developed, you may have been used to a more assertive partner who, more often than not, used to take much of the initiative. A number of the conditions considered in this book blunt initiative, and if you would like the sexual side of your relationship to continue, you may have to make a conscious decision to take more of this yourself now. This is perhaps particularly true for a carer looking after a person in the early stages of dementia.

Tackle treatable sources of irritation. Some aspects of your partner's behaviour which put you off the idea of sexual intimacy, such as aggression and incontinence, may be treatable. It is always worth taking some time to think about these things, rather than lumping all the problems together in one grey, shapeless mass that seems quite overwhelming, understandable though this is. Consequently, if the person you care for has one of the problems considered elsewhere in this book, try working through the relevant section to see if some action can be taken in that respect.

Make sure you have sufficient rest and respite care. Feeling continually tired and stressed is not conducive to switching on sexually. Are there any ways in which you can better organize your days so as to have more rest? Is there a friend or neighbour, or someone else in the family who could sit in while you are out for an hour or two, or help with some of the chores? Carers often feel very diffident about asking for this kind of help, and, as we have discussed, they also often feel that they have been abandoned by friends and family to the point that they never see them any more. If you say what specifically would help, you may just be pleasantly surprised by the response.

There is an old saying about absence making the heart grow fonder; it is very much to be doubted that this was coined with carers in mind, but it is certainly of relevance to your predicament. Regular respite care organized on a systematic basis may help in this respect.

Reconstrue behaviour. As mentioned earlier, it is important to try different ways of looking at something that irritates you about your partner's behaviour. If they make repeated and unwelcome sexual advances, rather than seeing this as their having become obsessed with sex, try to see it as one way in which they still know how to express their affection for you. Admittedly this is often easier said than done, but it is an important strategy in your day-to-day coping. It is facilitated by trying to put yourself in the other person's shoes, and will sometimes put quite a different complexion on something previously experienced as irritating.

Medication can be a useful adjunct to help with sexual difficulties, at various levels. Where there is a lack of sexual interest because of depression, antidepressant drugs may have a role in getting the ball rolling. In this case, it is wise to see this as only one component of therapeutic help. If *you* are the one who is depressed, it is particularly important not to rely on drugs as the only iron-in-the-fire of therapy, as counselling used in conjunction with drugs is likely to have better results, particularly in terms of keeping you free from depression in the future as well. Counselling is unlikely to help a person with severe dementia, but should definitely be considered for someone in the early stages of this illness, as it should be for someone with Parkinson's Disease, stroke or serious depression.

Medication can also have a valuable role in damping down libido where this is experienced as excessive, or in treating paranoid ideas where the partner makes constant accusations (unfounded!) concerning the carer's infidelity. With respect to the former, this is something of a delicate area, touching on the whole question of civil liberties and infringement of personal rights. But if this side of things is intolerable for you, it is worth exploring with the doctor who knows your situation best. When physical discomfort such as can arise from arthritis, for example, prevents sexual intercourse, a doctor may be able to prescribe pain-relieving medication.

When a relative needing care lives with you
Most of the situations discussed so far presume that your sexual relationship (or lack of it) is with a partner whom you care for. Different problems occur when the person needing care, perhaps an elderly relative, is living with you and your family. This may or may not be a situation of your own choosing; perhaps, for example, you are looking after a parent-in-law. To state the obvious, stress is likely to be higher when the situation is not at all what you would like, but one which you have accepted out of a sense of obligation or duty. Whether the situation is of your choosing or not, there are two primary goals to aim for:

1 That the caring role does not exhaust you, and leaves you with sufficient time and space for your personal life and interests.
2 That you and your spouse or partner have sufficient privacy for intimacy.

Caring can be exhausting, and if you are worn out at the end of the day you will be in no fit state to respond to your spouse's amorous attentions when they come in from work. Exhaustion can take many forms and your fatigue may be as much emotional as physical. If your day has been characterized by continual battles with someone you are caring for, it may be difficult to switch from resentment towards them to romance with your spouse. Yet what is clear is that if there is no romance with your spouse, you and your spouse are likely to feel taken for granted and resentful — assuming of course that this side of your relationship was one that was intact prior to the person needing care coming to live with you. Such a situation needs urgent attention. (Chapters 4 and 5, on coping practically and emotionally, are essential reading.)

Like politics, caring is the art of the possible, and compromise is often the only possible option. Compromise means a balance between the needs of you and your spouse or partner's and those of the person needing care. An arrangement where this person is living with you must leave sufficient space for your own private life. If this seems impossible it is essential to sit down and establish why. In most instances the word 'seems' is the appropriate one; a little (or, if necessary, a great deal of) thought will establish ways to achieve what you wish. A sitting service provided by a friend or member of the family, or by an official agency such as Crossroads (see Appendix I) during the day for an hour or two may make an appreciable difference to the way you feel in the evening when your loved one comes home. Although many carers stress the unavailability of this kind of relief, experience suggests that the biggest obstacle to achieving this and regular respite care is the carer's feeling guilty about accepting it and leaving the dependant. This area is addressed in some depth in Chapter 5, but suffice it to say here that this is part of what is meant by devoting a proper period of thought to the issue.

As important as having some emotional breathing space is the effort to tackle any problem behaviour of the person you care for, particularly any difficulties that are wearing you out with irritation. You share this need with the carer whose spouse or partner is the person they care for, and like them you need to consult the relevant section of this book; do not underestimate what can be done to ease frustrating problems; directed effort will make life easier in the area addressed, and may also have a quite profound effect on your personal life with your loved one.

Privacy as a goal can be difficult to obtain, particularly when caring for someone who is confused and who tends to wander in and out of rooms willy-nilly. Clear labelling of rooms, perhaps using a colour code if language has been lost, is important, as is consistent and firm management: a system where sometimes it is all right for this person to wander into your bedroom and at other times not is worse than useless; no intellectually impaired person can reasonably be expected to cope with this. Your bedroom is simply out of bounds, full stop. Consistency is an absolute necessity in any attempt to change behaviour.

When thinking about difficulties in your personal life with your spouse or partner in conjunction with those arising from having this person living with you, it is important to be realistic in your assessment of the development of the former. If these difficulties were there anyway, long before you needed to care for another person, the stress and fatigue associated with caring may well have aggravated the problem, but they did not cause it. Blaming them for a lack of marital intimacy in these circumstances may help ventilate some of your dissatisfaction, but does nothing to address the issue. To be frank about this, it is not uncommon for the caring of another person to become a convenient peg on which to hang all life's difficulties and, although this may be a painful exercise, it is better to give an area like this proper thought in terms of timing, basis and cause. At least then you have a better chance of tackling and overcoming the real problem.

Inappropriate sexual behaviour

Whatever difficulties may or may not exist in the relationship between carer and cared-for, there may be serious concerns about the possibility of inappropriate sexuality from a person with advanced senile dementia. A carer may worry about this person making sexual advances towards a relative, friend or child, by confusing these people with their spouse perhaps. A carer may worry about the person they care for removing clothing in public, or masturbating in inappropriate places. Clearly this is a highly emotive subject, and it is important to state at the outset that these sorts of problems rarely occur. Where they do happen, it is essential to try and respond calmly. Sometimes a little thought will show that the person you care for is not in fact 'exposing themselves' but, rather, is simply too hot and is forgetting social niceties, or has been taken short and again has forgotten that they are not in the appropriate place to relieve themselves. Explanation to others about the illness is vital, perhaps along the following lines: "Grandad has an illness that makes him very confused. He was probably very tired and ready for bed, and therefore simply started taking his clothes off, forgetting that he was still downstairs with other people." Use common sense. This might include using dresses, blouses and trousers which are difficult to undo — for the person you care for, not you! Where appropriate, distraction may do the trick, with the provision of something interesting to do. It is essential that other members of the family, including children, and friends who come into regular contact with you and the person you care for are educated about the illness and its effects, and respond to any problems of this nature in a matter-of-fact manner.

Medication can have a role when there are serious difficulties in this respect. For men, drugs such as medroxyprogestrone acetate can be prescribed to lower the production of testosterone. Sexual disinhibition in severe dementia has also been controlled successfully with a drug commonly used as a beta blocker, for example *Pindolol*, which takes effect quickly and has limited side-effects. Before taking this particular option, consultation with a specialist is essential.

Sex after a stroke
Resuming a sexual relationship after one partner has had a stroke can be a matter of some anxiety. People worry that the act of intercourse will bring on a further stroke, and apart from this anxiety there may be physical problems resulting from the stroke that make love-making difficult practically.

Before considering specific difficulties or anxieties that may be present, it is worth pausing for a moment to consider how comfortable you are about talking to your partner about worries or sexual difficulties. Whatever the cause, difficulties of this nature are always much easier to treat and, it is hoped, overcome when the two people involved are relaxed about talking to one another about their problems. The word 'their' is used here advisedly; a sexual difficulty involves two people, and even if the problem seems essentially to be that of one person, the partner's reaction to it can maintain or even aggravate the situation. Being able to talk calmly about it allows both to realize, for example, that a reluctance to have sex (perhaps because of a fear that it will precipitate another stroke) does not mean — as perhaps had been thought — that one spouse no longer finds the other attractive, or is having an affair! Being able to talk also facilitates finding out what ways of expressing intimacy and affection are possible, perhaps as an interim step towards resuming full intercourse. Where the person who has had a stroke can no longer talk clearly, they can still be encouraged to show their partner what they like. It is important to feel and be creative here, trying to let go of any inhibitions you may have had previously. This is in your home, in your private life. Perhaps you can find new ways to express and receive your affection for each other.

Immediately following a stroke, there may well be a number of problems about the mechanics of having sex. A weakness or paralysis on one side of the body will cause obvious difficulties. A man may have difficulty in achieving an erection, although this is likely to come about as much as a result of the tiredness and depression which commonly follow stroke as from any physiological reason *per se*. For similar reasons women may lose interest in the sexual side of their relationship, or find it more difficult to become aroused.

Just as being able to talk is important, so is being kind *to* the problem in the sense of not getting angry about the fact that you are having these difficulties. Anxiety and anger about the problem will interact with the sexual difficulty to make the situation massively worse; for example, being anxious about becoming aroused is hardly the best recipe for sexual excitement, and in fact is most likely to guarantee a lack of it. What often happens is that a problem comes about initially for fairly simple reasons, such as stress, tiredness or depression; it is then made much worse by the anxiety and anger associated with it; finally, it is perpetuated solely *because* of the anxiety and anger, the original stress and fatigue having passed. Gentle persuasion in this situation is likely to help; brute force will make things worse.

It is often a good idea for the non-affected partner to take the more active role. Experiment with different positions and different ways of giving each other pleasure (helpful literature is listed in Appendix II). Someone left with a one-sided weakness after a stroke may find it easier to make love if they lie on the weak side, freeing the unaffected side of their body. Make time for intimacy, choosing a moment when you both feel relaxed and not worn out. If difficulties persist, consult your doctor, who may be able to refer you to someone with counselling skills in this area.

Some medication that is prescribed to control blood pressure can itself cause sexual difficulties, and an alternative drug which controls blood pressure equally effectively but which does not have that effect may be found. A man who has had a stroke and now finds it difficult to achieve erections sufficient for intercourse can be helped by a variety of techniques, including splints, injections and, occasionally, surgery.

Let us return to the concern a stroke victim or their carer may have: that sex may now be risky, perhaps leading to another stroke. The only potential hazard in this situation is where high blood pressure has been a problem, and was perhaps implicated in the stroke itself. Where this is the case, it is likely that medication is being used to control blood pressure, and that your doctor is monitoring this regularly. Given this, there is no reason to restrict or stop your sex life unless you are specifically advised to do so by your doctor. Continuing an active and previously enjoyed sex life is far more likely to keep you healthy than to cause problems. If you do have serious anxieties about this, talk to the doctor who knows you best.

It is very common for a stroke to be followed by a period when the victim feels particularly emotional and, not uncommonly, quite depressed. This may well cause a stroke victim to have little real interest in the sexual side of the relationship, and this may persist for some time. Here it is essential to be patient, for some of this emotionality and depression may be a physical effect of the trauma the brain has experienced, and thus not easily treated by medication or counselling. For this reason, most doctors are reluctant to prescribe antidepressant medication for someone whose stroke has been very recent, say within the last couple of months. If these feelings persist beyond six months, it is certainly worth exploring the avenues discussed in the following section on depression.

When discussing people who care for victims of other conditions, mention was made of the need for honest thought to be given to the nature of their marriage before a disabling condition began. If, for example, the sexual side of the relationship was poor before a stroke occurred, it will be so now, regardless of any emotional or physical difficulties now present. In saying this, it is obvious that the strain of caring and the strain of coming to terms with disabilities may have an aggravating effect on a longstanding problem. This will usually become clear if counselling is sought, and this process may help the couple to agree on areas of their relationship which need some nurturing.

Depression

Helping generally

Here we will be looking at trying to help someone get to grips with their depression, rather than coping with your own, as carer, which is considered in Chapter 5. It is important to realize that true depression is a state of mind that many professionals see as an illness; it is not some kind of self-indulgent feeling of misery out of which the person could 'snap' if they had a mind to. As you may know all too well from your own experience, it is a frame of mind which in a sense paralyses you, robbing you of any zest for life. It is like a tremendous weight weighing you down, something that is miserably present for most of your waking hours: a 'black dog', as Churchill put it.

When faced with someone who is depressed, an instinctive urge is to keep asking "What's wrong?"

Someone with deep depression is unlikely to be able to give much in the way of a reply to this, and such replies as they can muster are unlikely to respond to everyday reassurance, ("It's all right; I know we've got enough money to manage"). As the carer, it is in general terms better to respond to the feeling itself (as one would comfort any distress) rather than simply to challenge it in a kind of intellectual way, even though you may be able to see that concerns and worries that are voiced are unrealistic. The problem comes, of course, when you are living with someone whose depression goes on and on for weeks, months and even years. Here, we are looking at some kind of amalgam of comfort, challenge of the distortions that occur in any depressed person's thinking, and the development of some kind of protective skin for yourself.

Part of trying to help someone with depression is to challenge the exaggeratedly negative view they have of themselves, reminding them of things that demonstrably confirm their worth. Similarly, depressed people overload themselves by setting unrealistic goals and standards; for example, the house has to be spring-cleaned from top to bottom, all in one go. Because this is impossible, they are defeated at the outset and thus tend not to start at all—hence what can come across as a lack of motivation, if not outright laziness. The way to help here is to encourage the setting of more realistic standards and the breaking down of the overall task into more manageable chunks.

Although we tend in life to assume that feelings follow directly from some event, this assumption misses out the important ingredient of thought. It is not just that someone keeps us waiting (event) that causes the miserable feeling, it is how we think about the event that leads to the feeling. So if our thought is "Their boss has kept them late again", the consequent feeling may be no more than irritation—as much for them as for ourselves. If, however, the thought is "They can't be bothered to be on time because I'm of little account", the feeling is likely to be very different. Research suggests that people prone to depression tend to have this latter kind of thought far more readily than others, and this presumably comes about because somewhere deep in the bones, perhaps as a result of childhood experiences, they know they *have* been treated as though of little account. Even leaving aside the question of a depression which has reached such an intensity as to be a clinical problem requiring professional help, there is of course a message in here for carers. If something the person you care for does, such as soiling their clothes (event), is thought of as 'selfish and disgusting laziness', your consequent feelings will be very different than if you think it through along the lines of 'he used to be a most fastidious and thoughtful man; this wretched illness'.

But to return to a state of serious depression in the person you care for, one of the problems is that this kind of negative and catastrophic thinking tends to run unchecked by the person who does it. Part of helping is to get people who are prone to depression to sit down and go systematically through the thoughts they had about a particular episode which led (on one particular occasion) to them feeling very down, and help them consider alternative thoughts about what happened. It is absolutely vital that they learn to challenge initial black-and-white thoughts ("She's late; I don' count") in this way, otherwise, like a car on a hill with no brakes, such thoughts tend to run chaotically out of control.

Another potent feature in depression is a feeling of helplessness; depressed people may see their personal world as impossibly awful, with no possible way to change it. With no visible lever to pull, they feel trapped. To return to an earlier idea, all they see is an impossibly high mountain to scale, so they conclude that it is not worth even taking the first step. An important start with anyone who is depressed is to get them to take some decision — any decision — about anything, however small, that they can do to improve their lot. This may be something as 'simple' as taking regular exercise. All fit people feel better after exercise, and a daily walk may give Richard a feeling of greater energy, as well as fresh perspectives after the four walls of his bedroom. Similarly, although appetite is usually impaired in depression, small but attractively presented and cooked meals may help challenge the tedium of life.

Many people who are depressed find it helpful to set themselves the routine of a daily timetable (which could include the daily walk and visit to the library, as well as necessary household chores), if need be written down. This saves the effort of thinking about what to do at 11am on a Thursday, and may help to get some activity going (almost any activity is better than none for a person suffering from depression).

We also need to talk about this person's anger (we will discuss yours in the next section). From a clinical perspective, it is axiomatic that depressed people are usually very angry people who have quite firmly sat on their feelings. Whereas most of us will make it clear, even if in a mild way, if someone has seriously irritated us, people prone to depression are usually quite unable to do this, and instead quite habitually fail to assert themselves, even if they have been treated quite rudely. In a sense this process fuels the negative picture they have of themselves anyway ("I am of no account") but there is often also a smouldering resentment that takes but a little for a therapist or empathic listener to discover. Accordingly it is important for depressed people to learn to assert themselves appropriately, and voice their feelings of resentment and hurt. As part of getting them to simply talk, can you encourage them to open up to a friend or kindly relation? This is suggested partly to give you a break and partly because you are unlikely to be able to provide all the listening that may be overdue.

People who suffer seriously from a life-long tendency to depression are in reality often badly wounded, having been brought up by parents who were highly critical or uninterested. This leaves them with very real doubts about their own worth, and thus a vulnerability to conclusions such as "I don't matter to other people." Unfortunately, no matter how lovingly they may be treated in later life, and that includes by you as husband or wife, the perennial doubt continues ("Your affection wouldn't last if you really knew what I am like").

In my clinical work with depressed people I work long and hard to persuade them to take up some creative interest, by way of which they may learn, eventually, to appreciate their own work and thus become, as it were, effective parents to themselves. It can take a lot of hard work to get the process going, but if it is mobilized it can begin to shift the person's view of themselves.

Clearly professional help is an avenue which should be explored when depression is serious or goes on for any length of time. Depression may often respond well to treatment, which may be an amalgam of medication and psychotherapy but very often takes some considerable time to take effect, hence the importance of not delaying too long before seeking advice. Depression often affects people in bouts, between which they 'surface' and seem quite well. Even after treatment, someone may remain vulnerable in this way, although, encouragingly, any further spells tend to be less severe as the victim seems to have learned a few tricks for coping.

The effect on you
Living with someone who is depressed is no joke. It is *depressing* for you, and will have a major impact on the practical side of your life (for example, with a spouse who never wants to go out or do anything) and on the way you feel emotionally. This may include your coming to feel listless and apathetic — and frankly very angry on occasion. This anger may in part be simply a reaction to the 'apathy' of the person you care for, but may also be a reflection of what they are feeling, for, while this may sound a trifle mystical, people seem vicariously to experience what another is experiencing, without any of this being put into words. Sometimes this may enable you to help the person you care for put some irritation they have been feeling into words, and thus be done with it; sometimes not.

To be blunt about this, given that all of the points considered above have been looked at in connection with the person you care for, and you have tried to see things from their point of view and done what you can to help, that person cannot simply be given a blank cheque. You will need to develop something of a protective skin and independent life for yourself. Make a point of having time to yourself every day; vigorously pursue your own interests and maintain friendships that you have. Learn to treat yourself to little luxuries, and do what you can to keep a reasonable quality of life for yourself.

Stroke

Coping generally

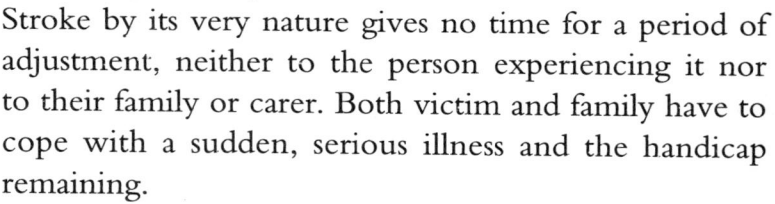

Stroke by its very nature gives no time for a period of adjustment, neither to the person experiencing it nor to their family or carer. Both victim and family have to cope with a sudden, serious illness and the handicap remaining.

In Chapter 3, we looked at the three typical times of crisis in connection with stroke, and the difficulties you will face as carer typically follow from the second and third of these: the recognition that there are going to be long-term handicaps and that you are now essentially on your own to deal with them. With regard to the latter, an important part of helping someone who has had a stroke is to ensure that you have been well taught about what rehabilitative techniques will help, be they physiotherapy, speech therapy or occupational therapy.

It is common for people who have had a stroke to become very emotional, bursting into tears frequently, seemingly without reason. This seems above and beyond the sadness one would naturally expect in anyone who suddenly cannot walk, move a hand, see or speak properly, and so on. It is perhaps connected with the physical upheaval the person has experienced, and the carer will need to learn not to continually disturb the sufferer with questions as to what is wrong.

It is also common for people who have had a stroke to become quite depressed for a period, perhaps lasting some months or even longer. Again, some aspects of this depression are perhaps related to the physical upheaval, but presumably not all. Stroke is an extremely frightening experience, and on top of this there is the process of adaptation to any residual handicap. This is bad enough for anyone, but clearly is going to have enormous impact on someone who cannot now pursue their previously enjoyed interests or occupation.

In any loss, perhaps, there comes a time when someone has to make a decision about having grieved enough, and then putting personal resources into picking up the pieces and making the best of life remaining — to put this plainly, by way of example, to decide what hobbies or interests *are* possible with one left hand, rather than weeping for those no longer available without two hands or the right one.

As with all penny lectures, it is easy to give advice when not experiencing the problem for yourself. But carers need to be mindful of the fact that the depression experienced by a victim of stroke does interfere with their capacity to see the glass as half-full rather than half-empty, and a degree of judicious firm but kindly insistence may be necessary to help this person maximize their remaining abilities. Part of this is a very deliberate encouraging of as much independence as possible.

In the section on 'Encouraging Independence' (pages 74-75) there was some discussion of the fact that, out of loving, empathic desire to help, a carer may try to spare a person the stresses and tedium of doing something that they themselves can do effortlessly in a moment. But nowhere is the idea that the long-term cost of this approach is too great truer than in the context of rehabilitation after stroke and, importantly in this connection, those stroke victims showing the best degree of recovery are those who go home and live alone; that is, who have to manage. And it has to be remembered that in the midst of their depression, robbed of early hopes that all would be well, all will 'come back', a stroke victim may feel capable of nothing, and thus feed into a carer's otherwise well-intentioned excessive support. It is not uncommon in this respect to see two people dovetailing very neatly in their behaviour; the one provides the complement to the other, albeit in what amounts to an unhelpful way. So part of helping the stroke victim is to guard against a natural impulse which may amount to excessive help, and also to fight the victim's tendency to see the mountain as impossibly high and to give up. Perhaps you can help them find a path with a gentler gradient, getting to the final summit by means of subsidiary, less daunting peaks. Having said all of the above, you should not let Richard struggle with tasks that are clearly beyond his capabilities. But in the assistance you offer, give only the essential minimum, leaving him to finish off what he is capable of.

A degree of personality change following stroke is also not uncommon. A previously capable, independent and resourceful man may become apathetic, withdrawn and passive. A quiet lady who had never been known to say 'boo to a goose' becomes hostile and rude. A degree of understanding about the experience the person you care for has gone through is essential here, so that they may *feel* this sense of understanding. This is particularly important given that the stroke victim may have lost, among other things, a degree of control over their feelings. But, having said this, it will be essential in this situation, as with depression, for you as carer to develop something of a protective skin for yourself. Part of this is to set firm and consistent limits about what you find acceptable, if necessary abruptly absenting yourself from time to time. Do bear in mind that some of the anger you see may be related to frustration at not being able to do things; it is painful to lose a skill (such as speech) which has previously been taken for granted, the importance of which only becomes clear when it is lost. A doctor may be able to prescribe medication to keep things on a more even keel.

Following a stroke, a person may feel embarrassed by their disabilities, and want to shut themselves away from social contact. Try not to let this happen. The stroke victim's view of themselves has already taken a severe jolt, and can do without the exacerbation of this situation that will surely follow if contact with friends and previously enjoyed interests is lost, even if this is self-inflicted. If they do shut themselves away from this contact, a hurdle is erected which becomes more difficult to overcome the longer it is there. Do try to build up their confidence, encouraging their efforts at rehabilitation and development of new interests which are now possible, and from which they can get a sense of their worth. You can help this by encouraging them to make their own decisions, and seeking their advice about problems you have.

Coping specifically

In the early days following a stroke which leaves *a weakness to one side of the body*, it is good practice to stand or sit on the 'good' side of their body, as vision on the weak side may also be adversely affected. The arm is commonly the most severely affected, and to prevent the complications of muscle spasticity or stiffness setting in it is vital that regular exercise is undertaken, and that the arm is positioned correctly at rest. If this does not happen and spasticity sets in, recovery will be all the more difficult (it may be limited anyway). It is therefore important to thoroughly understand the professional advice that will be given to you about this (probably from a physiotherapist), as most of what is done will have to take place at home. *Do not* rely on the person you care for's version of the advice given; be present with them on at least one occasion when advice is given.

Perhaps the most distressing and frustrating problem which can occur following a stroke is that of *not being able to communicate*. Moving beyond the initial phase of confusion that can badly affect many stroke victims and which tends to improve after a few days, there are two main types of language difficulty: dysphasia and dysarthria.

Let us first consider *dysphasia*. (You may also come across the term 'aphasia'. This is reserved by some professionals for cases where there is a complete inability to express or to comprehend language, as opposed to a disturbance in these functions.) This disorder itself takes two main forms. In the first, the sufferer has a marked word-finding difficulty — they know what they want to say, but cannot find the right word — and may also make grammatical errors. These people have insight into their difficulty, and get extremely frustrated with themselves. They may come to rely heavily on one word or phrase they *can* put their tongue to and use this endlessly.

The second group of people with dysphasia have no difficulty finding 'words', but in fact come out with a patter amounting to nonsense without any awareness that it is nonsense, looking baffled when we clearly do not understand them.

Dysphasic people are also often unable to understand language, whether it is spoken or written down. With mild forms of the disability, the subtle nuances of language may be lost.

Victims of a stroke who are left with dysphasia need a great deal of encouragement to use the language they do have, particularly those with insight into their difficulties who might otherwise withdraw into themselves out of embarrassment and frustration. Use short and simple sentences, speaking slowly and clearly — *not* loudly — they are not deaf! Use and encourage the use of mime and gesture to aid understanding, taking plenty of time and using pauses in your speech. People with dysphasia tend to tire easily through the effort of concentration.

The person with *dysarthria* speaks in a slurred and indistinct way, as if drunk. They understand language, both written and spoken, perfectly, and also use it correctly, but it is difficult for us to understand them. The problem here is that of control over the muscles of the lips, tongue and mouth used in the production of speech. Consequently someone with this disability may also have difficulty with chewing and swallowing. Fortunately this is a disability which tends to improve, particularly with the help of a speech and language therapist.

To help a stroke victim who has dysarthria, your speech should be normal; they have no difficulty with the comprehension of language. They should be encouraged to talk slowly and use short sentences to facilitate *your* concentration and understanding.

Whatever the nature of the communication difficulty, a good starting-point is assessment and guidance by a speech and language therapist; they will be able to advise you and the person you care for as to the exact nature of the problems and may well be able to suggest specific exercises to address these. In general:

1 Make sure that Richard can see you clearly, and that your face is not in shadow.
2 Where possible, only attempt important conversation in quiet surroundings: turn off the television or radio.
3 Get Richard's attention before attempting to talk to him.
4 Use gesture and clear facial expression as an aid to understanding, if possible pointing to what you are talking about.

5 Keep what you want to say short and to the point; do not flit rapidly from one topic to another.
6 Do not let yourself or anyone else talk about Richard as if he is not present; people can 'ask' him if he takes sugar in his tea by gesture. If you do not want your friend to visit again, find a friendly way to say this.

When you and the person you care for are with others, do try to help the person feel included socially, even if they clearly do not understand much or any of the conversation.

I feel strongly that anyone left with a severe disability in communicating with others should be firmly encouraged to take up some creative interest. This needs to be more than any old hobby to provide some light relief and distraction; rather what is needed is painting, pottery, music, writing (if this is intact) or some other way of producing something that only the person who has suffered a stroke would do in *that* way, and an activity which will ultimately provide a vehicle to express their feelings, and offer one way to help restore self-esteem.

7
The Carer's Journey

In the Beginning

LIFE IS not fair. You are no angel — never pretended you were — but by and large you have tried to lead a decent life. You do not deserve this. And you are not the cause of it either. This is a common misapprehension that carers suffer from: that in some way they may have contributed to or actually caused the difficulties experienced now by the person they care for — perhaps if they had not got angry that time; perhaps if they had cooked healthier meals; perhaps if they had stopped them drinking so much, smoking so much; perhaps if they had encouraged them to have more interests, to go out more, perhaps, perhaps …

Each carer's reaction to the difficulties of the person they look after is an individual one; tears are similar but different. This aspect is particularly important in a situation like this, coloured as it is by the particular relationship between carer and cared-for. We will consider this below, but for the moment, we will concentrate on what may be some of the common experiences in the journey carers make. After the initial sense of shock and disbelief, it is common to feel a sense of indignation: it is not fair. All the plans for the future, the hopes for retirement, all out of the window. The overriding feeling is one of loss, and the recurrent question is 'why?' Often this question will be particularly painful for someone with a religious belief: why has God allowed this? To deal with this dilemma, some will shrug fatalistically ("It is the will of God"). Others are less convinced:

> Fur hoffens we talkt o' my darter es died
> o' the fever at fall:
> An' I thowt 'twur the will o' the Lord, but
> Miss Annie she said it wur draäins.
> Tennyson, The Village Wife

Sometimes it is possible to explain why a disability occurs; very often it is not. Commonly people battered by misfortune know this deep down and their "Why me?" is an expression of protest and a plea for suffering to be shared and supported. Eventually, the essence of coping is to move on from the why to the how and the what: how do we get to grips with this problem; it is what we make of the situation that comes to matter most.

The Carer's Grief

When the light really does die, and a person's disabilities are so severe as to change them out of all recognition, the carer's overwhelming feeling is one of loss. Whilst they may not articulate it in this way, this loss in fact often comprises multiple losses: of companionship and friendship, a confidant with whom to share worries, a sexual relationship, financial security, the future they planned together (perhaps for their retirement years), recreational and social life and so on. Part of the peculiar challenge of your situation as carer is to manage your own real grief while at the same time continuing to maintain a loving kindness towards someone whose illness is the cause of this grief. By definition, this means that carers often have at the same time a number of feelings that are in many ways contradictory: anger and loving patience, resentment and pity. That these coexist, albeit uneasily, is quite a tribute to the carer and, I suppose, characterizes what it is to be human and care.

After someone has suffered a serious stroke or some years of dementia, it is common to feel that you, the relative, spouse or friend, have in some sense lost the person you have known for years or a lifetime. In a way you have, particularly if a once kind, gentle person has become rude and aggressive, or a capable, independent adult has become like a demanding, helpless child. Although we usually talk of bereavement when someone has died, the feelings you may experience over time are not dissimilar to those of the bereaved. There is a great deal that you have lost, although the person is still with you and perhaps in many respects quite 'well'. This is a tease and a cruel one. It is quite normal to experience a whole range of feelings, starting with disbelief (perhaps searching for a different diagnosis or magic cure), followed by anger — with those who gave the diagnosis, with those who are supposed to help, with books and information, like this, supposed to have helpful ideas which are in fact 'useless', with the person themselves ("He's always smoked—I told him and told him"), then by guilt ("Perhaps I should have spotted the signs, done this, done that"), and by a great sadness, not to mention sheer fatigue.

The carer's grief is always a peculiar, personal, individual experience, coloured by the nature of their relationship with the person they are now caring for over the years. It is often only after the loss that you as carer experience that the full nature of the relationship you had with this person becomes clear; you realize that they were, for example, your best friend and the person who was good at sorting out money concerns and any problems that came along. As well as working through all the painful feelings of grief you have, an essential part of your adjustment is learning to fill some of these gaps that have been left, often seemingly absurdly simple, like learning how to mow the lawn.

Having made an analogy with bereavement, it is important to recognize how you may have less support than someone who has, in fact, been bereaved. In a bereavement, there is the symbolic ritual of the funeral to help with a public recognition of the loss. Ideally this reminder of the bereaved's need for compassion helps to trigger the support of friends. *Your* loss, while real enough to you, particularly as the months go by, is less immediately visible to others. Because of this, you may struggle essentially alone with all manner of feelings.

Hope

Faced by any calamity, our initial reaction, beyond that of numbing shock, tends to be one of hope:

maybe there has been a ghastly mistake, maybe it is not that bad, maybe a cure will be developed. Carers become extraordinarily sensitive to the nuances of what is said to them in this context; one doctor or nurse says of a man who has had a stroke, "There may be quite a bit of improvement yet"; another that "He's probably made most of the functional improvement we're going to see." Of the lady who may have Alzheimer's Disease, one says "It begins to look as if it is Alzheimer's"; another, "Let's take one step at a time." This sensitivity to the nuances of any particular communication can work in a number of ways. Hopes of recovery or major improvement which initially may be very high—perhaps unrealistically so—may be fuelled in the early days perhaps by over-optimistic staff pronouncements or, importantly, what is *heard* as great optimism. In the emotionally highly charged early days of a trauma our attention and 'hearing' can be selective and sometimes inaccurate. Conversely hope, which we all need, can be dashed by what comes across as professional pessimism, informed as it is by a realization of the importance of not raising unrealistic hopes. In fairness to the professionals involved, it is of course extraordinarily difficult to get this balance right.

Anger

In any major loss, as some of the hopes evaporate, a typical, if not universal, feeling is one of anger. As with all types of anger, this needs a target, whether God ("Why me?"), medical staff ("They could have done more; could do more"), other members of the family who 'don't understand and don't help', the person you care for who has 'always smoked and never taken any exercise' or even the carer themselves ("I should have..."). Ideally, of course, the illness or disability itself becomes the target of this anger, as when, for example, Richard soils his clothes five minutes after being changed or when you have banged your head really badly on the cupboard door and he stares at you uncomprehendingly.

Part of the anger you feel may have to do with the reversal in roles that takes place: a man who has never set foot in the kitchen now has to do so to care for his wife; a son or daughter now has to care for a parent. Many of the disabilities considered in this book develop in late middle age or in the early years of retirement. A wife who was able to rely on an active, adventurous husband had planned with him to spend their retirement travelling and seeing something of the world, using the nest egg of their lifetime savings and visiting their daughter in Australia. His sudden, serious disabling stroke (or gradually developing depressive illness or dementia) send all of these plans out of the window, and to add insult to injury their savings end up being spent on residential care or converting the house to cope with his physical handicaps. The peak age of onset for Alzheimer's Disease is after the age of 80. This implies that carers, whether spouses or even sons or daughters, are likely themselves to be getting on in years. A mother whose children are off her hands and who has spent some years picking up a previous job and interests is suddenly faced with another 'child' in the form of a highly dependent adult. (Perhaps it is not even *her* parent.) It should be said that this can sometimes work well in practice, for example with a newly retired man who has felt at a loose end, whose now dependent wife gives him a sense of role again. Adjusting to this reversal of roles may be gradual, as when a person develops dementia or becomes depressed over a period of time, or be frighteningly sudden, as when a stroke occurs.

The feelings of initial hope and then anger have been articulated separately because they are clearly seen and perhaps universal. Much of the general sense of loss cannot be so clearly articulated but does, for example, often include feelings such as embarrassment. Going out with a person who constantly dribbles and talks gibberish, perhaps for a drink with friends, is not easy. Trips to the shops with Richard can become a nightmarish obstacle course, without him a rare luxury—although in that rare event, what about the anxiety and sense of dread: is he all right at home?

One largely unseen loss that many carers face is that of their social and recreational life. As their burden of care increases, and this may be slowly or abruptly, depending on the nature of the disability of the person they care for, contact with friends may be lost. Friends may well rally round in the early days, but *their* difficulty in knowing how to relate to their friend, coupled with their sense of embarrassment and fear of intruding into what is clearly a very private situation, may lead them increasingly to stay away. This may also happen in part because you have visibly difficult feelings about their *seeing* the change in your relationship. In many respects, people need to be alone with grief. Alas, the resentment that you nevertheless begin to feel when friends do, for whatever reasons, visit less is in turn sensed by them, and not unnaturally they are all the more inclined to stay away.

You, for your part, are less able to visit your friends. This may come about for a variety of reasons, from the simple practicalities of not having someone to sit with the person you care for to free you to go out, to a feeling that the person you look after cannot be 'inflicted' on your friends. Whatever the cause, few friendships survive a lack of nurturing by periodic get-togethers.

Just as any bereavement rarely affects one person only, so it is with this kind of loss. Other family members and friends have their sense of loss; their process of adjustment to make. Part of this process may be adjusting to losing you, the carer, who have perforce to spend so much time now caring for grandmother, father or whoever else it might be. Further to this, *their* relationship with the person you care for has changed irrevocably: our little friend Christine's grandad is not the grandad he was (see page 70).

Adjustment

This book started with a look at the process of coming to terms with a disability, and how the idea of acceptance can be used a little glibly (by those who have not had to suffer the experience). Nevertheless to come through some kind of process of adjustment *is* necessary, and perhaps part of the challenge of caring is being able to absorb the feelings of loss and anger into some kind of accepting forgiveness and to 'gather up the pieces left over so that nothing is wasted' (John 6:12). This, really, is the nub of it; although this book has looked at many of the problems faced by carers, and the anguish they suffer, there are often times of great closeness and tenderness, and 'nothing that creates such tenderness can be all waste' (P. Worsthorne, writing in the *Sunday Telegraph*, September 1990). The heart of caring is love, sharing the other's grief, absorbing their anger at the unfairness of it all, and by that love affirming their worth and purpose. There are, of course, times, when part of keeping the person you care for company in their grief will involve a degree of detachment on the part of the carer; becoming a 'nurse' for aspects of their care perhaps. Necessary as this is, it can fuel your distress as carer as well as that of the person you care for; the very basis of your relationship has changed. Perhaps in this there is some kind of 'balance of suffering' between yourself and the person you look after, but where the latter's insight is lost there may be a shift to a point where yours is the greater burden. In the midst of this, your lot is to:

1. Persevere with the grind of repetitive daily care;
2. Rejoice in the achievements of the person you care for, no matter how 'small';
3. Have the courage to accompany this person in their grief, their journey of disability;
4. Have the vision to believe that their losses, that your losses, provide the potential for gain.

When the Caring Ends

There are times when caring has to end; perhaps the person dies or it is not practical or emotionally possible for you to continue. This in itself is a further loss, particularly if caring has been something you have done for years. There may have been little time for interests or friends, now there is a huge hole, only a part of which was filled by looking after another person. This book has frequently stressed the need to preserve a life apart from caring; in part this has been in preparation for this day. If the time comes when it is no longer possible for *you* to be caring, allow yourself to be receptive to this advice.

8
Letting Go

SOME TIME was spent in the chapter 'Coping Emotionally' talking about guilt. In my experience, this is the most significant factor causing difficulty when the time comes for accepting, first, respite care, and then perhaps full-time residential care for the person you care for. Paradoxically guilt can be a major problem, albeit in different ways, both when the relationship between yourself and Richard has been good and when it has been poor over the years. When the relationship has, on balance, been a good one, the legacy of good feelings arising out of this helps to enable caring with a good heart: 'Each be other's comfort kind' (Gerard Manley Hopkins).

You want personally to give something back out of a sense of gratitude and continuing affection; it is not Richard's fault that he's now ill and needs help. This is what a large majority of carers feel; they set their shoulders to the wheel and try to make the best of things. Having said this, even when the relationship with Richard has, over the years, been good, it is not always easy. There may be some considerable conflict between what you want to do personally and other demands on your time. This is perhaps particularly true if you are wanting to care for an elderly parent at home, but are married and have your family to think of also. Our spouses do not necessarily share our tenderness for a parent; witness the popularity of in-law jokes! Conflict that can arise from this situation adds massively to the physical strain of caring. Not unnaturally, you will have thoughts such as "Is this such a good idea?" or "If only I could have a break." Then perhaps you remember Richard's earlier kindness to you, and feel overcome with guilt.

There is distress also in the different situation where the relationship between yourself and Richard has been poor over the years. It is more complicated, in that you will have a variety of reasons for caring at all. In part these may arise from a sense of reparation, making right now what could not before be made right; and in part they can come from a sense of guilt. These feelings are often accompanied by an appreciable degree of anger, and can become a millstone you carry in your daily life. As discussed in Chapter 5, caring now for a parent with whom you have had a difficult relationship in previous years is also particularly stressful. The nature of this stress may remain largely 'unseen', however, for example by other members of the family. Hence the not uncommon situation of a brother or sister feeling that things 'are not that bad'. Part of the difficulty with these kinds of emotions is that, although you have feelings of guilt, you carry on working hard at caring and may end up also feeling very angry with the person you care for and others around you. This is why it is so essential to recognize the point at which you need respite care, if not a permanent arrangement of residential care. It is not your fault or because of your inadequacy that this point has been reached; and it may be reached even though months or years earlier you gave a well-intentioned promise: "I'll never let you go into hospital." Events and difficulties can overtake and overwhelm anyone in a way impossible to foresee at the time when such promises are made.

This is a complicated area, but it is suggested that the simplest and best rule of thumb is that when the stage is reached that you are doing yourself more harm than you are doing good for the person you care for, the time has come for residential care. Caring full-time involves great sacrifice in many areas: loss of independence, restriction of social life, fewer opportunities to pursue personal interests to name a few. This has been a continuing price to be paid, and most carers pay it gladly, particularly if they can have a little recognition. But a point can be reached where these costs are minimal compared to those exacted on your health and emotional well-being.

One of the great difficulties about all of this is the potential for acrimonious argument between different members of the family; others, perhaps, do not see the person you care for as that difficult, and certainly see no reason why they cannot remain at home with you. Apart from anything else, this adds greatly to the sense of guilt the principal carer has, and also to the likelihood of a feeling of failure; many carers, sadly, feel that they have in some terrible way failed when that point is finally reached where they are not able to cope further at home. It should also be said that this can work the other way round, in that others in the family may have felt for a long time that "Richard should go into a home." Doubtless you will have weighed up this in many ways attractive, proposition, trying to disentangle their motives for saying this: they are right, they are fed up with an in-law they have never liked anyway living with them, they are wanting to ease their conscience about doing so little and leaving it all to you. Together with your deliberations in this respect, other members of the family arguing for the relative to go into permanent residential care can contribute to another feeling commonly experienced by carers in this situation, namely that they are 'abandoning' the person they care for.

Ideally it may be possible to sort all this out by talking with relatives, but not all families get very far by talking; you may simply have to do what comes to feel as the best for you, and of course the 'you' in this situation may very much include other important people, such as children or a spouse who have for so long missed out. Many may well feel very guilty about being the prime mover in making this kind of decision, but the time that you have spent caring gives you a great deal in the way of rights in this situation.

There are experiences beyond the reach of words. Sadness, bearable only if it has a positive meaning, unbearable now it has none:

To every thing there is a season,
and a time to every purpose
under the heaven;

A time to be born, and a time to
die; a time to plant, and a time to
pluck up that which is planted;

A time to kill, and a time to heal;
a time to break down, and a time to
build up;

A time to weep, and a time to
laugh; a time to mourn, and a time
to dance;

A time to cast away stones, and a
time to gather stones together; a
time to embrace, and a time to
refrain from embracing;

A time to get, and a time to lose;
a time to keep, and a time to cast
away;

A time to rend, and a time to
sew; a time to keep silence, and a
time to speak;

A time to love, and a time to
hate; a time of war, and a time of
peace.

(Ecclesiastes 3)

And, perhaps, a time to let go.

You will probably often know in your heart when this point is reached; Richard no longer recognizes you, and you no longer recognize him. Caring for what amounts to a stranger has become a grind almost bereft of meaning and you feel yourself little by little going under. Perhaps all that keeps you going is a sense of guilt and the expectations of others around you. Little by little your health and your life are slipping away. This is the time for others to take over. Not because they will do it better, but because it frees you to have a different relationship with Richard and also to have some life for yourself. Such a decision, rather than meaning 'putting him away' or 'abandoning' him can in fact mean putting back into your relationship a quality and affection which circumstances have driven out.

Appendix I

Useful Organizations

Age Concern England
Astral House
1268 London Road
London SW16 4ER
0181-679 8000

Age Concern Scotland
54a Fountainbridge
Edinburgh EH3 9PT
0131-228 5656

Age Concern Wales
91-93 Caerphilly Road
Cardiff CF4 4AE
01222 521052

Most areas have their own local group, some providing services such as relatives' groups and advice about welfare rights.

Alzheimer's Disease Society
2nd Floor
Gordon House
10 Green Coach Place
London SW2 1PH
0171-306 0606

Publishes a large number of helpful leaflets about this condition. The main central office will be able to advise about what local groups exist.

Benefits Agency
Benefits Enquiry Line: 0800 882200

A free, confidential telephone advice line for people with disabilities, their carers and representatives, offering general advice and information on benefits and disability organizations.

Carers' National Association
20-25 Glasshouse Yard
London EC1A 4JS
0171-490 8818

Offers a large number of helpful leaflets and information (free to carers) covering just about every conceivable topic of relevance to carers, including holidays, having a break, helpful gadgets and finding your way through the maze of social services benefits.

Citizens' Advice Bureau
The addresses of local branches are in the telephone directory. They offer help with availability of local ser-

vices, advice about welfare rights and specific problems.

Court of Protection
Stewart House
24 Kingsway
London WC2B 6JX
0171-269 7000

Crossroads
10 Regent Place
Rugby
Warwickshire CV21 2PN
01788 573653

A charity with over 200 local branches offering support to carers. Some branches offer a 'sitting' service with care attendants.

Huntington's Disease Association
108 Battersea High Street
London SW11 3HP
0171-223 7000

Social Services
The addresses of local offices are in the telephone directory. Social services provide a wide range of help, including day centres for the elderly and residential homes for respite care, and they can arrange for a social worker to help you.

The Stroke Association
CHSA House
123–127 Whitecross Street
London EClY 8JJ
0171-490 7999

Publishes a large variety of extremely helpful booklets explaining stroke illness and the psychological effects of this. Over 400 support groups are affiliated to CHSA, and these in turn often run 'Stroke Clubs' which people who have had a stroke can attend.

Note. These addresses were correct at the time of going to press. However, organizations do move or change telephone numbers. Your local Citizens' Advice Bureau should be able to provide you with current addresses of any organization that you may have difficulty contacting.

Appendix II

Helpful Books

Alzheimer's Disease Society, *Caring for the Person with Dementia — a Guide for Families and Other Carers*. A small booklet produced by the Society and available from them. This is an excellent, down-to-earth guide with practical lists on just about every problem that might crop up — both in the person you are caring for and in yourself. A good place to start.

* *Butler R N & Lewis M I*, *Sex After Sixty: A Guide for Men and Women in Their Later Years*, Hall and Co., 1977. (The paperback edition is called *Love and Sex After Sixty*.)

Gostin L, *Court of Protection*, Mind Publications. Mail Order Service, 4th Floor, 24-32 Stephenson Way, London NW1 2HD.

Hewer R L and Wade T, *Stroke: A Practical Guide Towards Recovery*, Prentice Hall, 1986.

A helpful guide which takes the reader through the reasons why a stroke occurs, the problems that can follow, and which offers practical advice about support and management.

* **Sandford C**, *Enjoy Sex In The Middle Years* (Positive Health Series), Optima, 1990.

Stokes G, *Managing Common Problems with Elderly Confused People (Aggression; Incontinence & Inappropriate Urinating; Screaming & Shouting; Wandering)*, Winslow Press, 1987, 1988.
Readable advice about understanding and treating these particular problems.

Woods R T, *Alzheimer's Disease: Coping With A Living Death*, Souvenir Press, 1989.
A comprehensive and empathic guide

* These books have very positive advice about the sexual side of the relationship in later life, although they do not specifically address some of the disabilities considered in this volume.

Index

Figures in **bold** refer to major sections

Acceptance 2, 3, 64
Activities
    encouraging 45
    failure-free 94
    loss of interest in 7
    needing help with **86**
Adaptation (to disability) 19, 127
Affection 7, 37
Age Concern 48, 150
Aggression **92-96**
    confrontation as trigger of 73
    in dementia **92-96**
Agnosia 95
Aluminium (as possible cause of Alzheimer's Disease) 9
Alzheimer's Disease **8-10**, 87, 107, 138, 139
Alzheimer's Disease Society 48, 55, 151
Anger
    carer's feelings of 60, 67, 94-96, **138-140**
    channelling constructively 98
    following a stroke 34-35
    from the person cared for 129

in dementia 7
   in depression 38, 123
   in Parkinson's Disease 12
   preventing episodes of 94
   safe outlets for 109
   with sexual difficulties 118
   with the person cared for 50, 67, 96
Anxiety
   about leaving the person cared for 140
   about sex after a stroke 116
   as trigger in wandering 88
   early Parkinson's Disease mistaken for 12
   in context of sexual difficulties 106, 118
Apathy
   in early dementia 8
   in Parkinson's Disease 12
   in the person cared for 71, 106
   the carer coming to feel 125
Aphasia 130
Arthritis 12, 19, 112
Assessment
   differentiating depression from dementia 22
   in early dementia 14-15
   of disability for level of benefit 54
   of eyesight 19, 99
   of eyesight difficulties following a stroke 19
   of language and communication problems 132
   of reason for marital problems 114
   of toileting difficulties 100-102
   professionals expertise in 42-48
Attention
   gaining 46, 85, 132
   in depression 39

in Parkinson's Disease 12
in sleep problems 92
when distressed 138
Attitude 38

Benefits 44, 53-55, 57, 151
Bereavement 21, 36, 85, 136-137, 141

Carer Support Groups 61, 103
Citizen's Advice Bureau 58
Clinging 29, 71, **87-89**
Clothing (managing) 98-100
Communication
    about sexual difficulties 105
    as a factor in toileting difficulties 101
    following a stroke 32, 132
    in dysarthria 132
    speech therapy to assist with 19, 46
Concentration
    and risk of accidents 53
    cause of fatigue (with respect to
        language difficulty) 131-132
    in dementia 7, 24
    occupational therapy help with 45
Confrontation **73-74**
Confusion
    as a trigger of anger 95
    at night 91
    following a stroke 130
    in cared-for people 71, 78
    in dementia 29, 84-88
    query about cause 42

Counselling
    about Huntington's Chorea 14
    clarifying reason for marital difficulties 119
    for depression 111
    for sexual difficulties 105–106
    for sexual difficulties arising from a stroke
        or disability 118
    seeking 41, 67–69
Court of Protection 57, 152, 154
Computerised axial tomogram (CAT Scan) 15
Crossroads 48, 52, 113, 152

Day Centre 44, 45, 152
Dementia **4–6**, 73–74, 78, 82–89
    associated with depression 20–21
    early signs of 6–8
    experience of 25–31
    main causes 8–14
    multi-infarct (arteriosclerotic) 10–11
    overview 14–16
    pseudo-dementia 22
    subcortical 12
Depression **20–23**, 106, 111, 118
    after a stroke 127–130
    effect of on carers 125–126
    experience of 35–39
    helping generally 120–125
Diagnosis **1–3**
    anger with 136
    basis of in dementia 14
    mistakes in 12
    of visual problems 47
Dignity 39, **72–73**, 95

Disorientation
  as cause of incontinence 99
  at night 91
  effect on relationship 107
Dressing 45, 48, 49, 54, 74, 97
Dysarthria 130, **132**
Dysphasia **130–131**

Electroencephalograph (EEG) 15
Embarrassment 140
Emotional Support **60–63**
  from community psychiatric nurse 47
  in depression 22
Energy 36, 123
Exercise
  after a stroke 18, 44, 130
  carer's need for 49–50, 69
  need for exercise in the person you care for 89
  to help with depression 123
  to help with sleep problems 90
Exhaustion 51, 71, 112

Family
  anger toward 67, 138
  burden to ix
  cared-for person's confusion about 85
  concerned 7
  effect of a stroke on 126
  effect of person being cared for on co-resident 112
  effect on 141
  excessively optimistic 35
  explaining cared-for person's difficulties to 94, 116
  feeling abandoned by 110

    feelings about residential care 146–147
    in context of Huntington's Chorea 14
    member as receiver 57
    need for support from 16, 51–52, 59, 69, 110
    needing to consider 145
    reluctance to accept problems 6
    talking to 61–62
Financial help 41, **53–55**
Forgetfulness **78–86**
    as a blessing 95
    as a cause of accidents 53
    as early feature of dementia 7–8
    assessing reasons for 42
Frustration
    as a cause of a cared-for person's restlessness 89
    cared-for person's 129
    following a stroke 33, 35, 130
    in context of memory problems 80
    in early dementia 29
    inability to share 61
    sharing with other carers 103

Guilt
    about accepting respite care 50–52, 114, 144
    arising in context of poor relationship 146–147
    as part of grief 60, 137
    as sole reason for caring 149
    cared-for person's feeling of 27–28
    carer's feelings of 63–69, 72
    easing 109
    family's feelings of 62
    following anger 94
    in context of sexual problems 105

Health
>breakdown of in carers 64-65
>contrast of cared-for person to 73
>in context of sex after a stroke 119
>of carers 45, **48-50**, 68-69, 149
>protective of multi-infarct dementia 10

Hearing impairment 83
Hemianopia 19, 33
Hope
>carer's early 137-138
>following a stroke 31, 34-35, 128

Hopelessness
>carer's feelings of 60, 97-98
>in depression 36
>with respect to incontinence 100

Huntington's Chorea **13-14**
Huntington's Disease Association 14, 152

Impotence 117-119
Incontinence **96-102**
>continence adviser 46
>following a stroke 19

Independence
>carer's loss of 146
>change in 39
>encouraging **74-75**, 128

Initiative
>loss of as early sign of dementia 8
>taking more 109

Insight
>cared-for person having 84, 96, 131
>cared-for person not having 107, 108, 142
>in early dementia 7, 11, 29, 73

Insomnia **89–92**
Irritation
　after a stroke 32, 33, **130–133**
　as a cause of aggression 93
　in caring 67, 114
　influence on sexual relationship 110
　person you care for facing in others 31
　person you care for feeling 93, 125

Language Problems
　following a stroke 33
　in context of forgetfulness 81
　in context of incontinence 97, 101
　in context of wandering 114
　in dementia 9, 12
　role of speech and language therapist 46
Legal arrangements **56–58**

Medication
　following a stroke 18, 19
　for blood pressure; possible cause of sexual
　　difficulties 118
　for depression 23, 125
　for insomnia 89
　for sexual problems **111–112**, 116
　ineffective 119
　monitoring the effects of 47
　side-effects of tranquillizing 91
Memory (see also forgetfulness) **78–86**
　of person you care for 22, 30
　in dementia 5, 7, 11, 24–28, 30
　in Parkinson's Disease 12
　poor; impact on person you care for 95

problem of as a feature in relationship difficulty 107
problem of as a feature of incontinence 102
Motivation
   in context of incontinence 99
   lack of in depression 36, 120-121
   not implicated in person you care for's problems 24
   person you care for's lack of 39, 71, 106
Multi-infarct dementia **10-11**

Overload 38, 93, 121

Paranoid ideas 112
Parkinson's Disease **11-13**
Personality change 9, 12, 71, 129
Power of attorney 57
Pre-senile dementia 6, 13

Relationship
   between carer and partner 134, 137, 142, 144-145, 149
   sexual 102-109, 112-115, 117-120
Rejection 37, 108
Reminiscence 85
Resentment 67, 82, 113, 124, 136, 140
Residential care 47, 56, 102, 139, 144
   time for **146-147**
Respite care **50-52**
   and carer's well-being 59
   arranging 43-44
   feeling guilty about accepting 64-65, 114
   influence on relationship 110
   signs of needing 51

Restlessness 88
Risk
   following a stroke 19
   of a further stroke 18
   of depression 21
   of Huntington's Chorea 13-14
   of sex after a stroke 119
   of suicide in depression 21
   minimizing in the home **53**

Sexual difficulties **102-120**
Sleep problems — see under insomnia
Social Services 48, 51, 54, 61
Standards, 22, **63-66**, 75, 87, 121
Stress x, 8, 12, 27, 64, 66, 69, 88
   importance of sufficient rest 110
   minimizing **75-76**
   when prior relationship with person now cared for
      was poor 145
   with respect to sexual difficulties 106, 108, 112,
      115, 118
Stroke **16-20**
   coping generally **126-130**
   coping specifically **130-133**
   experience of **31-35**
   sex after **116-120**
Stroke Association (The) 48, 153

Transient Ischaemic Attack (TIA) 18
Toileting difficulties 48, 54, 81, **96-102**

Wandering **87-89**